Sewing ACCESSORIES

Martha Pullen
PUBLICATION
Sew Beautiful

The Martha Pullen Company
Founder: Martha Pullen, Ph.D.
President: Kathy McMakin
149 Old Big Cove Road
Brownsboro, Alabama 35741
800.547.4176 • 256.533-9586
www.marthapullen.com
www.sewbeautifulmag.com

Publications Director

Leighann Lott

Editor

Charlotte Potter

Copy Editors

Betsy Iler

Amelia Johanson

Karen Pyne

Book Designer

Vicki Ramsey

Photography

Jennifer & Company

Photo Styling

Leighann Lott

Vicki Ramsey

Color Correction

Clark Densmore

Illustrators

Angela Atherton

Kris Broom

Katina Logan

Contributing Designer

Charlotte Gallaher

Hoffman Media, LLC
President: Phyllis Hoffman
Executive Vice-President/COO: Eric W. Hoffman
1900 International Park Drive, Suite 50
Birmingham, Alabama 35243

Contents

Introduction

Well-appointed rooms hold accessories that complement an overall theme, and your sewing room need not take exception to this basic rule of home décor; however, sewing room space often is limited, so accessories must be as functional as they are fashionable. This charming book, the most recent Martha Pullen / Sew Beautiful publication, offers lovely sewing accessories that will help you organize your workspace as you beautify it. Pincushions, chatelaines, and scissors sleeves keep your most essential sewing tools conveniently at hand while smattering your favorite room in the house with style. We even help you take sewing room style with you – to classes, waiting rooms, and everywhere you might steal a few minutes to indulge in fine stitching. With projects like a linen sewing purse (page 6) and an elegant sewing organizer in silk and linen (page 42), you'll find yourself looking forward to packing up a sewing project so you might merely unfold an adequately stocked – but well decorated – sewing room anywhere at all!

BASIC SEWING SUPPLIES

- Dressmaker shears
- Small embroidery scissors
- Ruler or tape measure
- Rotary mat, cutter and rotary ruler
- Point turner
- Iron and ironing board
- Press cloth
- Sewing machine (with embroidery capabilities if embroidery is desired)
- Wash-out marker or chalk marker
- Lightweight construction thread to match fabrics and trims
- Hand sewing needles (#6 or #7 sharps or #7 or #10 betweens)
- Size #70 and #80 universal machine needles for construction
- Size #75 machine embroidery needle for embroidery
- Bodkin set with needle-style bodkin and flat bodkin
- Point turner
- Temporary spray adhesive
- Fray Block™
- Glass head pins
- Small sticky dots for marking pieces (available from office supply store)
- Tissue paper for tracing patterns and templates

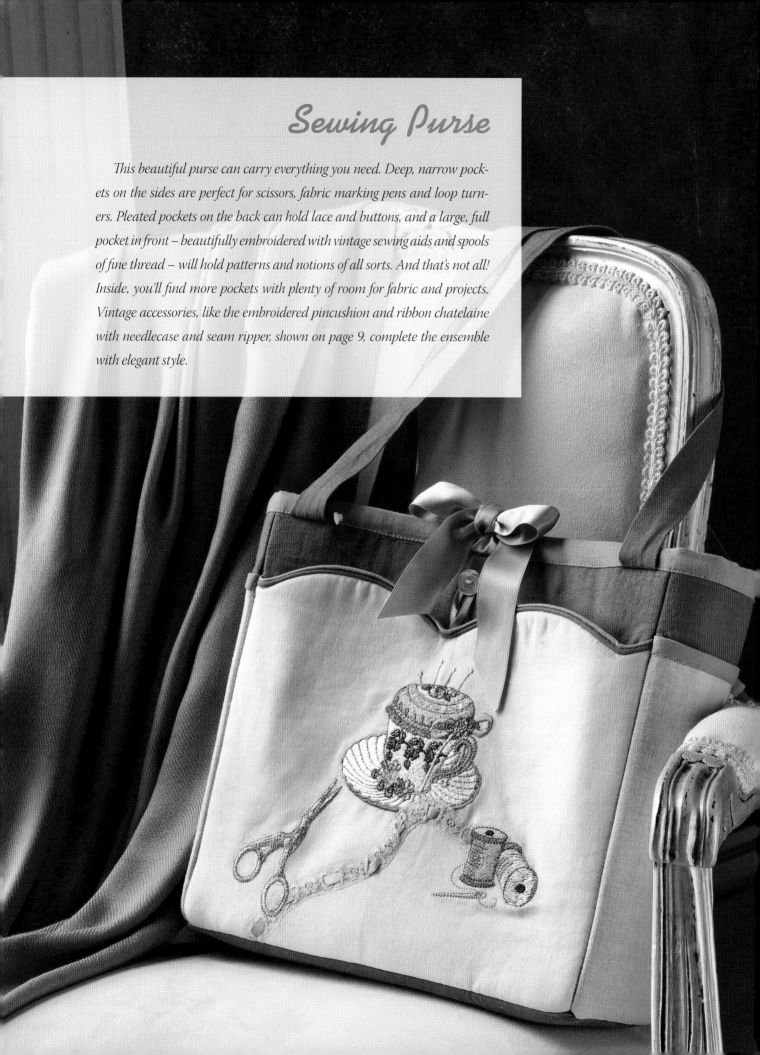

Sewing Purse

This beautiful purse can carry everything you need. Deep, narrow pockets on the sides are perfect for scissors, fabric marking pens and loop turners. Pleated pockets on the back can hold lace and buttons, and a large, full pocket in front – beautifully embroidered with vintage sewing aids and spools of fine thread – will hold patterns and notions of all sorts. And that's not all! Inside, you'll find more pockets with plenty of room for fabric and projects. Vintage accessories, like the embroidered pincushion and ribbon chatelaine with needlecase and seam ripper, shown on page 9, complete the ensemble with elegant style.

Please read through
all directions before
beginning.

Supplies

- 2/3 yard linen blend (white) (43/44"-wide)
- One yard linen blend (lavender) (43/44"-wide)
- 3/4 yard linen blend (sea green) (43/44"-wide)
- Floriani Stitch N Shape® (see cutting for sizes)
- Floriani Heat N Sta Fleece® (13" square)
- 1/3 yard 5/8"-wide ecru lace beading for pocket front embellishment
- 1/3 yard 1/4"-wide Vintage Gold silk satin ribbon for front pocket embellishment
- 1/8 yard 1/8"-wide Vintage Gold silk satin ribbon for front pocket button loop
- 3/4 yard 1"-wide Vintage Gold silk satin ribbon for purse ties
- Three 5/8"-wide (16 mm) 2-hole pearl buttons
- 1-1/3 yards baby piping cord
- Lightweight tear-away stabilizer
- Invisible thread
- 60-wt. thread to match lace beading
- White 60-wt. thread for construction

- Lavender 60-wt. thread to match linen blend for construction
- Darr Piping Magic Ruler
- Small sticky dots for labeling pieces (found in office supply stores)
- Lace shaping board
- Basic sewing supplies

- Robison-Anton® 40-wt. rayon embroidery thread in following colors:
  - 2582 Bone
  - 2314 Satin Wine
  - 2590 Hot Peony
  - 2241 Palm Leaf
  - 2232 Ecru
  - 2423 Pale Orchid
  - 2202 Olive
  - 2586 14 Kt. Gold
  - 2279 Spruce
  - 2382 Pastel Blue
  - 2206 Baby Blue
  - 2424 Cachet
  - 2501 Petal Pink
  - 2509 Bitteroot
  - 2516 Aqua Pearl
  - 2525 Heron Blue
  - 2434 Tropic Blue
  - 2224 Beige
  - 2336 Amber Beige
  - 2573 Pewter
  - 2433 Ultra Blue
  - 2571 Platinum
  - 2297 Snow White
  - 2264 Maize

Additional Supplies for Pincushion and Chatelaine

- Excess white linen blend will be sufficient for making Floral Dress Pincushion
- An additional 2/3 yard of 1/4"-wide Vintage Gold silk satin ribbon will be needed for chatelaine tool "cords"
- 7/8 yard of 5/8"-wide Vintage Gold silk satin ribbon for chatelaine neck "cord"
- One 1/4"-wide (8 mm) shank-style pearl button (chatelaine will button onto purse above front pocket)

Templates

Front Pocket Template Part A and B (page 62-63)

Embroidery Designs

Martha Pullen's *Sewing Accessories* embroidery CD was used to create embroideries and chatelaine for this project. (designs sb1711; sb1722; sb1719; sb1727; sb1725; sb1701; sb1709)

Cutting

Label all pieces with designated letter on sticky dot. Letters will be referenced during construction. All measurements are given width by length.

From white linen blend, cut the following (refer to cutting guide, page 69):
- Two 13" squares for front pocket and lining (A)
- One 20" x 8-1/2" rectangle for back pleated pockets (B)
- Two 5" x 8-1/2" rectangles for side pockets (C)

From lavender cotton linen blend, cut the following (refer to cutting guide, page 69):
- Two 3" x 23" strips for purse straps (D)
- Two 12" x 10-1/2" rectangles for purse front and back (E)
- Two 5" x 10-1/2" rectangles for purse sides (F)
- Two 12" x 7-1/4" rectangles for

front and back lining pockets (G)
- Two 5" x 6-1/2" rectangles for lining side pockets (H)
- One 1-1/2" x 23" strip of bias for front pocket piping (I)
- One 5" x 12" rectangle for purse bottom (J)

From green linen blend, cut the following (refer to cutting guide, page 70):
- One 36" x 2-1/2" strip for purse binding (K)
- One 32" x 2" strip for pocket bindings (L)
- Two 12" x 10-1/2" rectangles for front and back lining (M)
- Two 5" x 10-1/2" rectangles for lining sides (N)
- One 12" x 5" rectangle for bottom lining (O)
- One 1-1/2" x 23" strip of bias for front pocket piping (P)

From Stitch N Shape®, cut the following:
- Two 11-1/2" x 10-1/4" rectangles for purse front and back (Q)
- Two 4-1/2" x 10-1/4" rectangles for purse sides (R)
- One 4-1/2" x 11-1/2" rectangle for purse bottom (S)

Cut one 13" square of Heat N Sta Fleece®.

Ribbon will be cut as needed.

Directions

Pocket Embroidery and Embellishment

1. Fold and mark horizontal and vertical center of one front pocket (A) *(fig. 1)*.

2. Using Front Pocket Template, mark centers and directional arrows for each of three designs *(fig. 2)*.

3. Mark lace shaping lines *(fig. 3)*.

4. Stabilize, hoop and embroider design sb1711, Cup and Saucer, using colors and stitch sequence given on embroidery CD inside cover *(fig. 4)*.

5. Remove from hoop and place on lace shaping board.

6. Shape and stitch lace beading onto linen blend as follows:

    a. Begin pinning lace at one end along outermost curves of shape *(fig. 5a)*. Lace on inside curves of shape will be wavy. Place pins at an angle. ***NOTE:*** *Shaped lace will "travel" on top of embroidered saucer. End of lace will be under thread spools embroidery. Opposite end of lace will run off lower edge of pocket.*

FIGURE 1

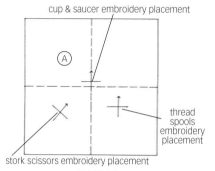

cup & saucer embroidery placement

thread spools embroidery placement

stork scissors embroidery placement

FIGURE 2

lace shaping lines

FIGURE 3

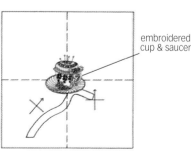

embroidered cup & saucer

FIGURE 4

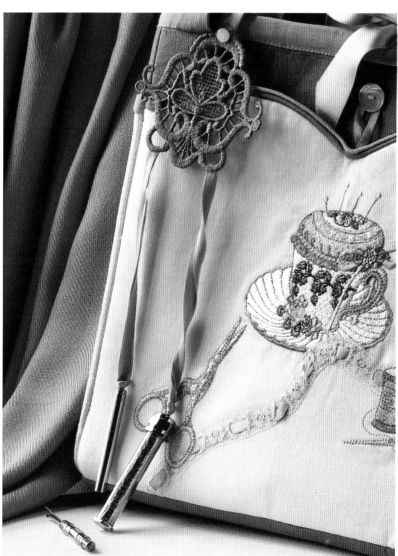

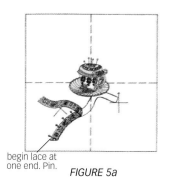

begin lace at one end. Pin.

FIGURE 5a

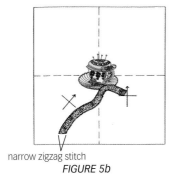

narrow zigzag stitch
FIGURE 5b

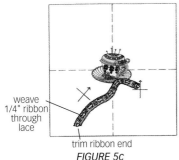

weave 1/4" ribbon through lace

trim ribbon end
FIGURE 5c

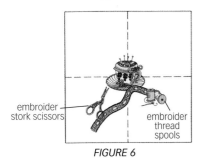

embroider stork scissors

embroider thread spools

FIGURE 6

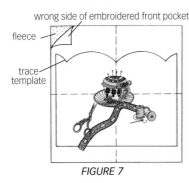

wrong side of embroidered front pocket

fleece

trace template

FIGURE 7

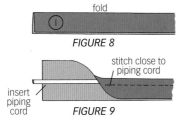

fold
FIGURE 8

stitch close to piping cord

insert piping cord

FIGURE 9

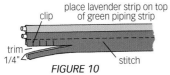

place lavender strip on top of green piping strip

clip

trim 1/4"

stitch

FIGURE 10

b. Pull uppermost thread in lace heading along inside curve to make lace lie flat. Lightly press lace. Re-pin through lace and fabric only and remove fabric from board.

c. Using lightweight thread to match lace, stitch along each lace heading using a narrow zigzag (L=1.5-2.0; W=1.5-2.0) *(fig. 5b).*

d. Cut a l2" length of 1/4"-wide silk satin ribbon. Thread bodkin with ribbon and weave through lace beading. Press ribbon flat. Trim ends of ribbon even with ends of lace *(fig. 5c).*

7. Stabilize, hoop and embroider design sb1719, Thread Spools, using stitch sequence given on embroidery CD inside cover. Be sure to hoop piece with arrow facing up. Embroidery will cover end of lace beading and ribbon *(fig. 6).*

8. Stabilize, hoop and embroider design sb1722, Stork Scissors, using stitch sequence given on embroidery CD inside cover. Be sure to hoop piece with arrow facing up. Embroidery will overlap lace beading and ribbon *(see fig. 6).*

9. Remove excess stabilizer. Rinse piece to remove markings. Allow to dry and press embroidery side down on fluffy towels.

10. Remark horizontal and vertical center of embroidered 13" square.

11. Place piece onto Front Pocket Template, matching vertical and horizontal center lines. Mark top scalloped line as well as bottom and side cutting lines *(fig. 7).* Do not cut out at this time.

12. <u>Lightly</u> fuse fleece to wrong side of embroidered front pocket according to manufacturer's directions *(see fig. 7).*

13. Cut length of piping cord in half.

14. Fold lavender bias strip (I) in half lengthwise, wrong sides together, and finger press *(fig. 8).*

15. Open strip and place one length of piping cord in center of strip. Refold strip with cord inside snug against fold *(fig. 9).*

16. Using a piping foot or zipper foot, stitch close to cord *(see fig. 9).*

17. Repeat steps 14 - 16 for green bias strip (P) and remaining piping cord *(see fig. 9).*

18. Place lavender piping strip on top of green piping strip with corded portion of lavender piping lying just under corded portion of green piping *(fig. 10).*

19. Using a zipper foot, straight stitch through all layers close to cord of lavender piping. This will create a strip of double piping *(see fig. 10).*

20. Using a piping ruler, trim seam allowance of double piping to 1/4" *(see fig. 10).*

21. Clip seam allowance of piping every 1/8" to 1/4" *(see fig. 10).*

22. Place raw edge of piping to drawn scalloped line on pocket front, right sides together. Straight stitch double piping to pocket front along previous stitching line (stitching line closest to raw edge of piping) *(fig. 11).*

23. Pull fleece away from fabric above stitched scallop. Trim fleece very close to stitching. Do not cut fabric *(fig. 12).*

24. Place remaining front pocket (A) (lining) and embroidered pocket front right sides together.

25. Stitching from wrong side of embroidered pocket front, straight stitch layers together along visible scalloped stitching line *(fig. 13).*

26. Trim away excess fabric 1/4" from stitching. Clip curves and points *(see fig. 13).*

27. Turn lining to wrong side of embroidered pocket front. Press well.

28. Pin layers together and trim along side and bottom cutting lines *(fig. 14).* Set lined pocket aside.

Creating Pleated Back Pocket

1. Fold back pocket (B) in half to measure 10" x 8-1/2". Crease *(fig. 15).*

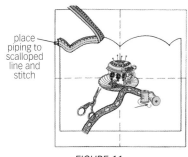

FIGURE 11

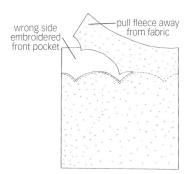

FIGURE 12

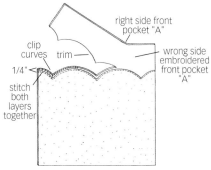

FIGURE 13

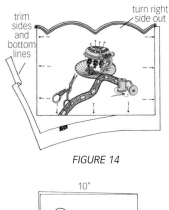

FIGURE 14

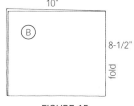

FIGURE 15

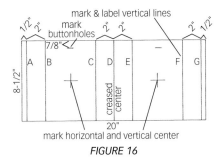

FIGURE 16

mark & label vertical lines
mark buttonholes
7/8"
mark horizontal and vertical center
creased center
20"
8-1/2"

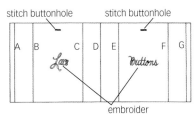

stitch buttonhole   stitch buttonhole
Lace   Buttons
embroider

FIGURE 17

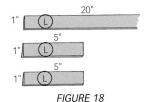

20"
1"
5"
1"
5"
1"

FIGURE 18

20" strip
stitch
wrong side back pocket

FIGURE 19a

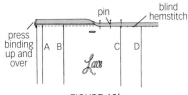

press binding up and over
pin
blind hemstitch
Lace

FIGURE 19b

match Line B to Line A
pin
Lace

FIGURE 20

match Line C to Line D
Lace   Buttons

FIGURE 21

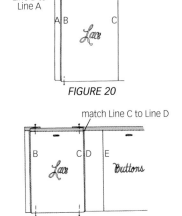

2. Unfold. Mark and label vertical lines according to *figure 16*. Line D will be creased center.

3. Measure and mark horizontal and vertical center of each large section as shown *(see fig. 16)*.

4. Stabilize and hoop fabric. Embroider design sb1727 at one center mark and design sb1725 at other marked center *(fig. 17)*. Remove excess stabilizer and press fabric well.

5. Stitch a horizontal buttonhole for a 5/8" button 7/8" from top raw edge of pocket piece and centered between lines B and C. Stitch a second buttonhole in same manner between lines E and F. See marked lines for buttonholes on figure 16. Cut buttonholes open *(see fig. 17)*.

6. Fold 32" x 2" pocket binding strip (L) in half lengthwise and press. From this length cut a 20" strip and two 5" strips *(fig. 18)*. Discard excess strip. Set 5" strips aside for side pockets.

7. Place 20" strip to top edge (wrong side) of back pocket (B) matching raw edges.

8. Straight stitch with 1/4" seam allowance *(fig. 19a)*.

9. Press binding strip up and over seam allowance to front of pocket, matching fold of binding to seam line. Pin in place *(fig. 19b)*.

10. Using invisible thread and blind hemstitch (L=1.0-1.5; W=1.5-2.0), stitch folded edge of binding in place *(see fig. 19b)*. Press well.

11. Create pleated pockets as follows:

    a. Fold piece wrong sides together at Line B. Match Line B to Line A, right sides together. Pin in place *(fig. 20)*.

    b. Fold piece wrong sides together at Line C. Match Line C to Line D, right sides together. Pin in place *(fig. 21)*.

c. Fold piece wrong sides together at Line E. Match Line E to Line D, right sides together. Pin in place *(fig. 22)*.

d. Fold piece wrong sides together at line F. Match Line F to Line G, right sides together. Pin in place *(fig. 23)*.

12. Baste pleats in place along lower edge. Set pleated back pocket aside.

Creating Side Pockets

1. Using side pockets (C) and 5" folded pocket binding strips, place one strip to top edge (wrong side) of one back pocket, matching raw edges.

2. Straight stitch with 1/4" seam allowance *(fig. 24a)*.

3. Press binding strip up and over seam allowance to front of pocket. Pin in place *(fig. 24b)*.

4. Using invisible thread and blind hemstitch (L=1.0-1.5; W=1.5 - 2.0), stitch folded edge of binding in place. Press well *(see fig. 24b)*.

5. Repeat steps 1 - 4 for remaining side pocket. Set pockets aside.

Creating Lining Pockets

1. Locate two front and back lining pockets (G) and two side lining pockets (H).

2. Along each top edge *(refer to figure 25)* turn a double 1/4" hem to wrong side of each pocket. Straight stitch in place and press well.

3. Locate two front and back lining (M) pieces and two lining sides (N).

4. Place wrong side of created lining pocket pieces to right side of lining pieces, matching bottom and side raw edges.

5. Straight stitch pockets to lining pieces 1/4" from sides and bottom *(fig. 26)*.

6. Divide pockets into smaller pockets if desired *(see figure 26)* by drawing vertical lines and stitching along lines. Backstitch at top edge of each divided pocket stitching line for added security.

7. Lining pockets and lining pieces will now be treated as one layer for construction. Set lining pieces aside.

Creating Purse Straps

1. Fold one purse strap (D) in half right sides together to measure 23" x 1-1/2".

2. Straight stitch long side of folded strap with a 1/4" seam allowance *(fig. 27a)*. Press seam open *(fig. 27b)*.

3. Turn strap right side out. Center seam along back of strap and press strap well *(fig. 28)*. Set strap aside.

4. Repeat steps 1 - 3 for remaining strap.

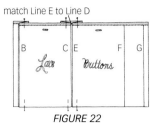

FIGURE 22

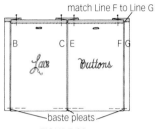

FIGURE 23

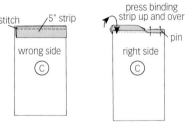

FIGURE 24a   FIGURE 24b

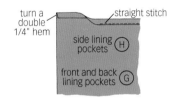

FIGURE 25

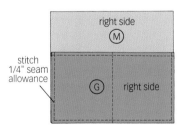

FIGURE 26

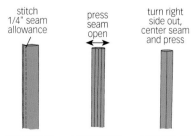

FIGURE 27a   FIGURE 27b   FIGURE 28

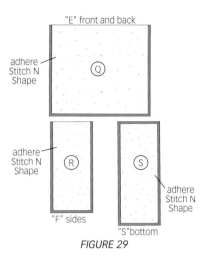

"E" front and back

adhere Stitch N Shape

Q

adhere Stitch N Shape

R

S

adhere Stitch N Shape

"F" sides

"S"bottom

FIGURE 29

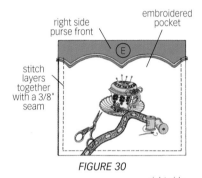

right side purse front

embroidered pocket

E

stitch layers together with a 3/8" seam

FIGURE 30

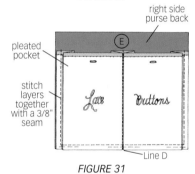

right side purse back

E

pleated pocket

stitch layers together with a 3/8" seam

Lace   Buttons

Line D

FIGURE 31

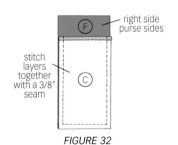

right side purse sides

F

stitch layers together with a 3/8" seam

C

FIGURE 32

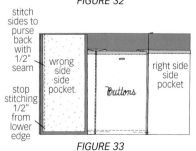

stitch sides to purse back with 1/2" seam

wrong side side pocket

right side side pocket

stop stitching 1/2" from lower edge

Buttons

FIGURE 33

Purse Assembly

1. Using temporary spray adhesive, adhere Stitch N Shape® pieces (Q, R and S) to wrong sides of purse front, back, sides and bottom. Note that top edges will be even on front, back and side pieces. There will be 1/4" of excess fabric along sides and lower edge of each piece and on all sides of purse bottom piece (*fig. 29*).

2. Place lining side of front embroidered pocket to fabric side of purse front (E) matching sides and lower edge. Straight stitch pocket to purse front with a 3/8" seam (*fig. 30*). This seam should barely catch edge of Stitch N Shape®.

3. Place wrong side of back pleated pocket to fabric side of purse back (E) matching sides and lower edge. Straight stitch pocket to purse back with a 3/8"

seam (*fig. 31*). This seam should barely catch edge of Stitch N Shape®.

4. Pin center of pleated pocket to purse back. Straight stitch along Line D (*see figure 31*) to create two pleated pockets. Do not stitch through folds of pocket. Backstitch at top binding to secure.

5. Place wrong side of side pockets (C) to fabric side of purse sides (F) matching sides and lower edge. Straight stitch pockets to purse sides with 3/8" seam (*fig. 32*). This seam should barely catch edge of Stitch N Shape®.

6. With right sides together, straight stitch sides to purse back with 1/2" seam, matching binding on pockets. Do not catch folds of pocket in stitching. Stop stitching and backstitch 1/2" from lower edge (*fig. 33*). This will make it easier to attach purse bottom.

7. With right sides together, straight stitch sides to purse front with 1/2" seam, matching binding on side pockets to piping on front pocket. Stop stitching and back stitch 1/2" from lower edge *(fig. 34)*.

8. Straight stitch purse bottom (J) to purse front, back and sides, stitching one side at a time and back stitching at each corner to secure *(fig. 35)*. Set purse aside.

9. Straight stitch lining sides (N) to lining front and back (M) (pocket sides together). Stop stitching and backstitch 1/2" from lower edge *(see figs. 33 and 34)*. This will make it easier to attach bottom lining.

10. Straight stitch bottom lining (O) to front, back and side linings, stitching one side at a time and back stitching at each corner to secure *(see fig. 35)*. Set lining aside.

11. Fold 1/8"-wide ribbon in half and hand tack to lining side of front pocket (centered) *(fig. 36)*.

12. With loop extended above pocket, mark a button placement onto purse front. Hand stitch a 5/8" button at mark *(fig. 37)*. Slip ribbon loop around button to close pocket *(see finished drawing)*.

13. On pleated back pockets, mark button placements behind buttonholes. Hand stitch a 5/8" button at each mark *(fig. 38)*. Button pockets closed *(see finished drawing)*.

14. Position handles, right side of handle to right side of purse, 1/4" from each corner seam on purse front and purse back. Baste handles in place 1/4" from top edge *(fig. 39)*.

15. Cut 1" wide ribbon into two equal lengths. Pin one length of ribbon at center top edge of purse front and purse back. Baste ribbon in place 1/4" from top edge *(fig. 40)*.

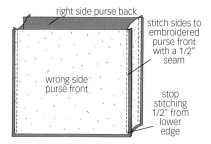

FIGURE 34

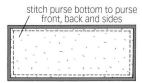

FIGURE 35

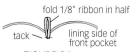

FIGURE 36

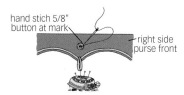

FIGURE 37

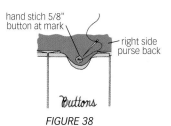

FIGURE 38

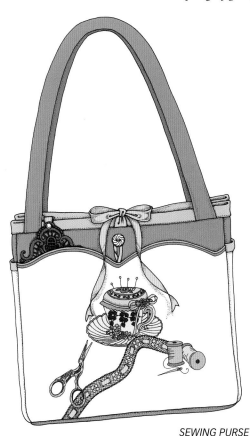

SEWING PURSE
FINISHED DRAWING

FIGURE 39

FIGURE 40

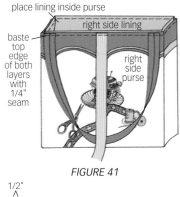

place lining inside purse

right side lining

baste top edge of both layers with 1/4" seam

right side purse

FIGURE 41

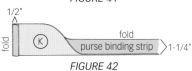

1/2"

fold

fold

K

purse binding strip

fold

1-1/4"

FIGURE 42

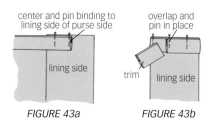

center and pin binding to lining side of purse side

overlap and pin in place

lining side

trim

lining side

FIGURE 43a   *FIGURE 43b*

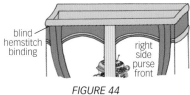

blind hemstitch binding

right side purse front

FIGURE 44

16. With purse right side out and lining turned wrong side out, place lining inside purse. Match corner seams and top edge. Baste top edge of purse and lining together 1/4" from raw edges *(fig. 41)*.

17. Fold one short end of purse binding strip (K) to wrong side 1/2" and press. Fold binding strip in half to measure 1-1/4" wide. Press well *(fig. 42)*.

18. Begin at center of one purse side and pin finished end of binding to lining side of purse matching raw edges *(fig. 43a)*. Cut excess binding 1/2" past beginning finished end of binding, overlapping two and pin in place *(fig. 43b)*.

19. With 3/8" seam allowance, straight stitch through all layers around top of purse. Press binding strip up and over seam allowance to front of purse. Pin in place.

20. Using invisible thread and blind hemstitch (L=1.0-1.5; W=1.5-2.0), stitch folded edge of binding in place on purse front *(fig. 44)*. Press well.

Optional: Topstitch binding close to fold using thread to match binding.

Floral Dress Pincushion

Refer to directions included with *Sewing Accessories* embroidery CD to embroider and construct Floral Dress Pincushion (design sb1700). Colors were used from supply list to coordinate pincushion with purse.

Freestanding Lace Chatelaine

Using 1/2"-wide silk satin ribbon for neck "cord" and 1/4"-wide ribbon for tool "cords," stitch Freestanding Lace Chatelaine (*Sewing Accessories* embroidery CD, design sb1709). Robison-Anton® color #2424 (cachet) was used for the sample. Attach 1/4"-wide (8 mm) shank-style button beside handle on purse front. Top of chatelaine will button to purse *(see finished drawing)*. Ribbons and tools may be slipped into pocket for carrying *(see purse finished drawing)*.

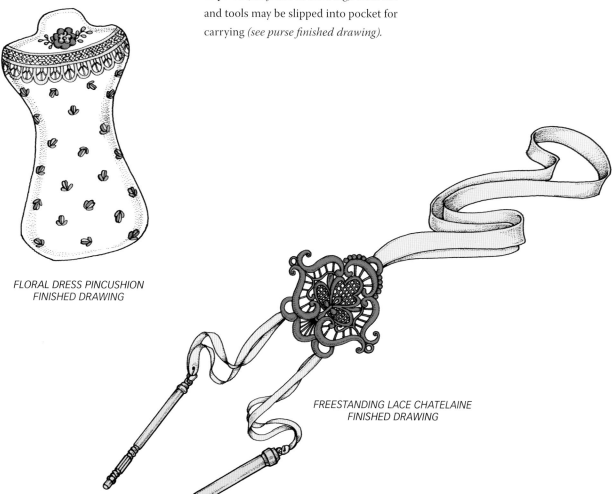

FLORAL DRESS PINCUSHION
FINISHED DRAWING

FREESTANDING LACE CHATELAINE
FINISHED DRAWING

Sewing Wallet

Banish idleness and make the most of stolen minutes in waiting rooms and car lines at the elementary school with this pretty and practical sewing wallet. With all of your tools and threads handy, and a small hand project tucked inside the pocket, you'll welcome those opportunities to take a few stitches, relax and enjoy your handiwork. And just think how much faster you will finish projects when you can work on them anywhere with ease!

Please read through all directions before beginning.

This sewing wallet was made to coordinate with the *Sewing Purse* (directions found on page 6).

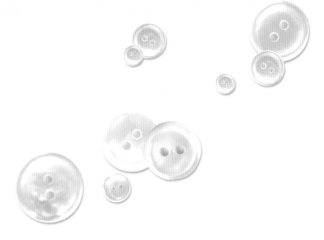

Supplies

- 1/4 yard cotton linen blend (white) (43/44"-wide)
- 1/3 yard cotton linen blend (lavender) (43/44"-wide)
- 3/8 yard cotton linen blend (sea green) (43/44"-wide)
- Floriani Heat N Sta Fleece® (5-1/2" x 8-1/2" piece)
- 1/2 yard 5/8"-wide cotton edging trim for pocket embellishments
- 1/2 yard 1/8"-wide gold silk satin ribbon for scissors tie and button loop
- One 5/8"-wide (16 mm) shank-style pearl button
- Lightweight tear-away stabilizer
- Invisible thread
- Walking foot for sewing machine (optional)
- Edge joining foot for sewing machine (optional)
- 60-wt. thread to match trim
- White 60-wt. thread for quilting
- Lavender 60-wt. thread for construction
- Small sticky dots for labeling pieces (found in office supply stores)
- Lace shaping board
- Basic sewing supplies
- Robison-Anton® 40-wt. rayon embroidery thread in following colors:
    - 2264 Maize
    - 2586 14 Kt. Gold
    - 2224 Beige
    - 2571 Platinum
    - 2573 Pewter
    - 2382 Pastel Blue
    - 2206 Baby Blue
    - 2516 Aqua Pearl
    - 2582 Bone
    - 2232 Ecru
    - 2297 Snow White
    - 2260 Hot Pink
    - 2590 Hot Peony
    - 2202 Olive
    - 2279 Spruce

Cutting

Label all pockets with designated number on sticky dot. Numbers will be referenced during construction. All measurements are given width by length.

From white cotton linen blend, cut one 8" x 11" rectangle.

From lavender linen blend, cut the following:
- One 8" x 11" rectangle for backing
- Two 8" x 5-3/4" rectangles for pockets #2 and #5
- One 4-1/4" x 8-1/2" rectangle for pocket #3
- One 4-1/4" x 5" rectangle for pocket #4
- One 6" x 5" rectangle for pocket #6

From sea (green) cotton linen blend, cut the following:
- One 9" x 11" rectangle for pocket #1
- One 2-1/2" x 36" strip for wallet binding

Cut one 8" x 11" rectangle of fusible fleece.

Ribbon and trim will be cut as needed.

Embroidery Designs

Martha Pullen's *Yesteryear* embroidery CD was used to create embroideries for this project. (designs mpc0124; mpc0125)

Color Sequence for Embroidery

Design mpc0124, Scissors, Etc.
- 1: 2264 Maize
- 2: 2586 14 Kt. Gold
- 3: 2224 Beige
- 4: 2571 Platinum
- 5: 2573 Pewter
- 6: 2573 Pewter
- 7: 2382 Pastel Blue
- 8: 2206 Baby Blue
- 9: 2382 Pastel Blue
- 10: 2516 Aqua Pearl
- 11: 2582 Bone
- 12: 2232 Ecru
- 13: 2573 Pewter

Design mpc0125, Pincushion, Etc.
- 1: 2297 Snow White
- 2: 2232 Ecru
- 3: 2586 14 Kt. Gold
- 4: 2260 Hot Pink
- 5: 2590 Hot Peony
- 6: 2571 Platinum
- 7: 2573 Pewter
- 8: 2202 Olive
- 9: 2279 Spruce
- 10: 2571 Platinum
- 11: 2571 Platinum
- 12: 2571 Platinum
- 13: 2571 Platinum
- 14: 2573 Pewter

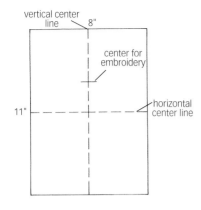

vertical center line

8"

center for embroidery

11"

horizontal center line

FIGURE 1

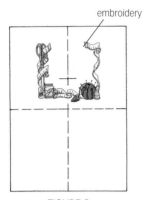

embroidery

FIGURE 2

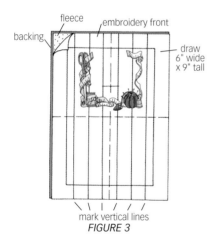

fleece

embroidery front

backing

draw 6" wide x 9" tall

mark vertical lines

FIGURE 3

Directions

Embroidery

1. Fold and mark vertical and horizontal centers of 8" x 11" white cotton linen blend *(fig. 1)*.

2. Mark center for embroidery designs in one of the following manners *(refer to finished drawing for placement)*:

Option #1

a. Combine the two embroidery designs in your embroidery software, overlapping designs to create a combined design measuring 4-1/8" wide.

b. Print a template of combined designs. Combined design should measure no more than 4-1/8" wide.

c. Center template horizontally using drawn vertical center line as a reference. Place lower edge of template 1/2" from horizontal center line.

d. Mark center of combined design onto rectangle as shown *(see fig. 1)*.

e. Stabilize, hoop and embroider combined design *(fig. 2)* using color sequence given on page 19. Colors given will coordinate with Sewing Purse.

Option #2

a. Print a template of each embroidery design.

b. Position each template onto top half of 6" x 9" drawn rectangle. Overlap templates until design measures 4-1/8" wide.

c. Center combined template horizontally using drawn vertical center line as a reference. Place lower edge of combined template 1/2" from horizontal center line.

d. Mark center for embroidery for each design.

e. Stabilize, hoop and embroider each design separately using color sequence given above. Colors chosen will coordinate with Sewing Purse.

3. Remove stabilizer from back of fabric and rinse to remove blue marks. Press piece well, embroidery side down, on fluffy towels.

4. Center and fuse fleece to wrong side of embroidered rectangle.

5. Re-mark vertical and horizontal center of piece on fabric side.

6. Place backing rectangle behind fleece and adhere with temporary spray adhesive *(fig. 3)*.

7. Complete Channel Quilting as shown on page 21, if desired.

8. Measuring from horizontal and vertical center of piece, draw a 6" wide by 9" tall rectangle onto fabric *(see fig. 3)*. Embroidery design will fall in top half of rectangle.

9. Cut out piece along marked lines *(refer to fig. 4)*. Set piece aside.

Channel Quilting (Optional)

a. Using vertical center line as a reference, mark lines 1" apart according to figure 3. Skip over embroidered design.

b. Thread machine needle with invisible thread or 60-wt. white thread. Thread bobbin with 60-wt. lavender thread.

c. Straight stitch (L=3.0) along marked lines to quilt, skipping over embroidered area *(fig. 4)*. ***NOTE: A walking foot may be used.***

Creating Pockets

Pocket #1

1. Fold 9" x 11" rectangle in half to measure 9" x 5-1/2". Press *(fig. 5)*.

2. Fold in half again to measure 4-1/2" x 5-1/2". Crease *(fig. 6)*.

3. Open last fold so rectangle measures 9" x 5-1/2" again. Mark center crease *(fig. 7)*.

4. Measure 1/2" on each side of center line and draw vertical lines *(see fig. 7)*.

5. Using thread to match cotton linen blend, straight stitch (L=2.0) along each marked line *(fig. 8)*. Set pocket aside.

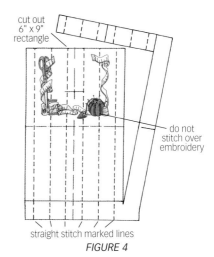

FIGURE 4

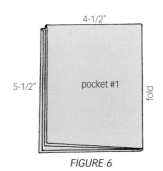

FIGURE 5

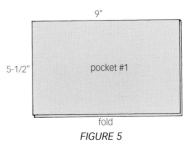

FIGURE 6

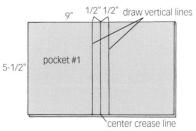

FIGURE 7

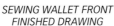

SEWING WALLET FRONT FINISHED DRAWING

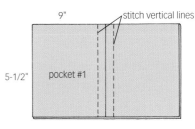

FIGURE 8

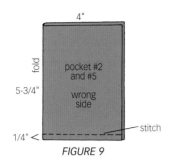

4"

fold

pocket #2
and #5

wrong
side

5-3/4"

1/4" < ----- stitch

FIGURE 9

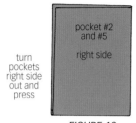

pocket #2
and #5

right side

turn
pockets
right side
out and
press

FIGURE 10

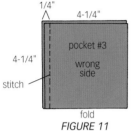

1/4"
∧
4-1/4"

pocket #3

wrong
side

4-1/4"

stitch

fold

FIGURE 11

pocket #3

right side

turn
pocket
right side
out and
press

FIGURE 12

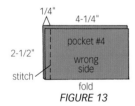

1/4"
∧
4-1/4"

pocket #4

wrong
side

2-1/2"

stitch

fold

FIGURE 13

pocket #4

right side

turn
pocket
right side
out and
press

FIGURE 14

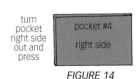

3"

fold

pocket #6

wrong
side

5"

pocket #6

right side

turn
pocket
right
side
out
and
press

stitch
1/4" <

FIGURE 15   *FIGURE 16*

Pocket #2 and #5

1. Fold each pocket (#2 and #5) in half, right sides together, to measure 4" x 5-3/4" *(fig. 9)*.

2. Straight stitch one 4" end on each pocket with a 1/4" seam allowance *(see fig. 9)*.

3. Turn pockets right side out and press *(fig. 10)*. Set pockets aside.

Pocket #3

1. Fold pocket #3 in half, right sides together, to measure 4-1/4" square *(fig. 11)*.

2. Straight stitch one 4-1/4" side, with a 1/4" seam perpendicular to fold *(see fig. 11)*.

3. Turn pocket right side out and press *(fig. 12)*. Set pocket aside.

Pocket #4

1. Fold pocket #4 in half to measure 4-1/4" x 2-1/2" *(fig. 13)*.

2. Straight stitch one 2-1/2" side, with a 1/4" seam perpendicular to fold *(see fig. 13)*.

3. Turn pocket right side out and press *(fig. 14)*. Set pocket aside.

Pocket #6

1. Fold pocket #6 in half to measure 3" x 5" *(fig. 15)*.

2. Straight stitch one 3" side, with a 1/4" seam perpendicular to fold *(see fig. 15)*.

3. Turn pocket right side out and press *(fig. 16)*. Set pocket aside.

Embellishing and Layering Pockets

1. Place pocket #3 on a flat surface with raw edges at bottom and to your left.

2. Cut a strip of trim 1/4" longer than top folded edge of pocket.

3. Pin trim to top edge of pocket with scallop extended. Turn end of trim under 1/4" at finished side of pocket *(fig. 17)*.

4. Using thread to match trim or invisible thread, straight stitch very close to straight edge of trim. An edge joining foot is great for keeping edge of trim and needle aligned *(fig. 18)*. Reposition needle to stitch in desired position.

5. Stitch a second line of stitching near top portion of trim catching pocket in stitching *(fig. 18)*.

6. Place pocket #2 on a flat surface with fold at your right and seam at top. Pin pocket #3 to pocket #2 matching sides and lower edges *(fig. 19)*.

7. Repeat steps 2 - 5 to attach trim to pocket #4 *(see figs. 17 and 18)*.

8. Pin pocket #4 to pocket #3/#2 matching sides and lower edges. This three-piece unit will be called the left unit. Topstitch along right hand side to attach pockets #3 and #4 to pocket #2 *(fig. 20)*.

9. Place pocket #6 on a flat surface with fold at top and seam to your right.

10. Repeat steps 2 - 5 to attach trim to top edge of pocket *(fig. 21)*.

11. Place pocket #5 on a flat surface with fold at top and raw edges to your left.

12. Pin pocket #6 to pocket #5 as shown *(fig. 22)*.

13. Mark division lines for pocket #6 as shown *(see fig. 22)*.

14. Choose a triple straight stitch on your machine. Thread machine needle with a contrasting embroidery thread (we used one to match trim) and thread bobbin with lightweight sewing thread.

15. Stitch along drawn pocket lines, through all layers, backstitching at top of trim to secure. Also stitch pocket #6 to pocket #5 close to finished edge *(see fig. 22)*.

16. Triple straight stitch along folded edge of pocket #5. This two-piece unit will be called the right unit *(see fig. 22)*.

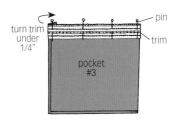

FIGURE 17

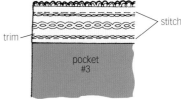

FIGURE 18

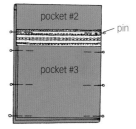

FIGURE 19

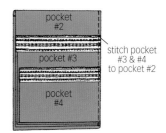

FIGURE 20

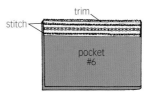

FIGURE 21

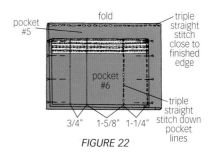

FIGURE 22

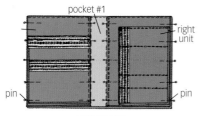

FIGURE 23

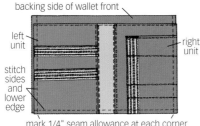

backing side of wallet front

left unit

right unit

stitch sides and lower edge

mark 1/4" seam allowance at each corner

FIGURE 24

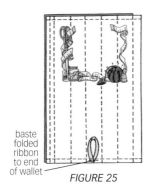

baste folded ribbon to end of wallet

FIGURE 25

1/2"

fold

wrong side

2-1/2" binding fold

FIGURE 26

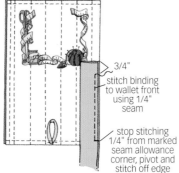

3/4"

stitch binding to wallet front using 1/4" seam

stop stitching 1/4" from marked seam allowance corner, pivot and stitch off edge

FIGURE 27

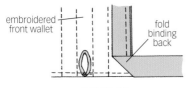

embroidered front wallet

fold binding back

FIGURE 28

17. Replace machine needle with construction thread. Place pocket #1 onto a flat surface with fold at top. Pin left and right units onto pocket #1 matching raw edges at each side and bottom edge *(fig. 23)*.

18. Straight stitch very close to top edge (folded edge of pocket #1) *(see fig. 23)*, attaching top edges of left and right units to pocket #1.

19. Pin completed stack of pockets to backing side of wallet front, matching sides and lower edge. Straight stitch sides and lower edges with a scant 1/4" seam allowance *(fig. 24)*.

20. With wallet pocket side facing up, mark 1/4" seam allowance at each corner *(fig. 24)*.

Binding

1. Cut a 4-1/2" length of 1/8"-wide ribbon. Fold ribbon in half to form a loop.

2. Center loop at unembroidered end of wallet, matching raw edges. Baste in place *(fig. 25)*.

3. Fold one short end of 2-1/2" wide binding strip to inside 1/2" and finger press. Fold binding strip in half lengthwise, wrong sides together, to measure 1-1/4" *(fig. 26)*. Press well.

4. With wallet embroidered side up, begin stitching (1/4" seam) binding to edge of wallet approximately 3/4" from folded end of binding *(fig. 27)*.

5. Stop stitching 1/4" from side at marked seam allowance corner. Lift machine foot with needle down, pivot and stitch through seam allowance off edge of wallet *(see fig. 27)*.

6. Remove from machine. Fold binding back on itself at pivot forming a diagonal fold from end of stitching to corner of sewing wallet *(fig. 28)*.

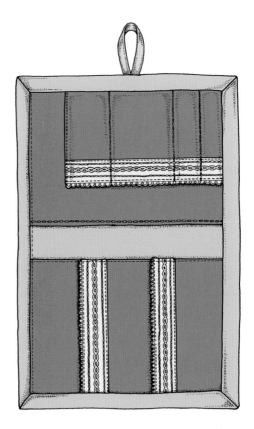

SEWING WALLET INSIDE FINISHED DRAWING

7. Fold binding again aligning bottom of wallet and raw edge of binding. the second fold will be at side of wallet. Pin in place *(fig. 29)*.

8. Resume stitching at 1/4" repeating steps 5 - 7 for remaining corners.

9. When you reach finished end of binding, cut away excess binding 1/2" past end of beginning binding *(fig. 30)*.

10. Slip cut end of binding inside folded end of binding *(see fig. 30)*.

11. Continue stitching binding to wallet.

12. Fold binding to pocket side of wallet, adjusting mitered corners. It may be necessary to trim corner seam allowances slightly. This will reduce bulk and allow miters to lie flat. Pin binding in place *(fig. 31)*.

13. Hand stitch binding to pocket side of wallet just covering stitching *(see fig. 31)*. Use a whip stitch or a blind hemstitch.

Finishing

1. Fold wallet closed with pockets on inside.

2. Fold ribbon loop to front of wallet and mark button placement inside loop *(fig. 32)*.

3. Hand stitch button to front of wallet *(fig. 33)*. Do not stitch through pockets.

4. Open wallet and designate a section on pocket #6 to hold small embroidery scissors.

5. Fold remaining 1/8"-wide ribbon in half. Crease. Open and hand stitch crease to pocket #5, 5/8" above designated pocket opening *(fig. 34)*.

6. Ribbon ends will be run through handles of embroidery scissors and tied into a bow.

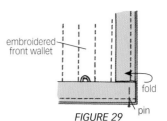

embroidered front wallet

fold

pin

FIGURE 29

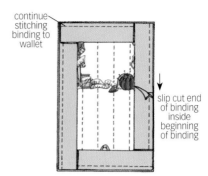

continue stitching binding to wallet

slip cut end of binding inside beginning of binding

FIGURE 30

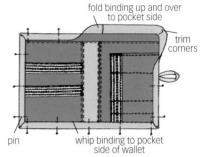

fold binding up and over to pocket side

trim corners

pin

whip binding to pocket side of wallet

FIGURE 31

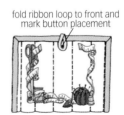

fold ribbon loop to front and mark button placement

FIGURE 32

hand stitch button

FIGURE 33

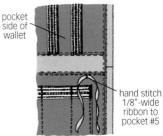

pocket side of wallet

hand stitch 1/8"-wide ribbon to pocket #5

FIGURE 34

The Well-Stocked
Sewing Station

Chairside Pincushion

Here is a perfectly ingenious chairside stitching accessory! This handy sewing aid securely holds eight spools of thread around an embroidered pincushion that is lovely enough to be mistaken for home décor! Two linen napkins, tacked together to form pockets, keep your threads neat and organized. When a color runs out, replacing it is a simple matter of untying the hidden elastic band that keeps them in place, tucking a spool into place and tying the band up again. The decorative silk pincushion has ample room to hold all the pins you'll ever need, and a bit of pretty ribbon dresses it up so much, no one will realize it's actually a tool!

Supplies

- Two ecru 8" square hemstitched linen napkins*
- 1/4 yard silk dupioni (candy pink)
- 3/4 yard 5/8"-wide ruffled miniature rose ribbon with ruffle (coral)
- 1-1/4 yard 1/8"-wide silk satin ribbon in your chosen color (sage shown)
- 3/4 yard 1/8"-wide baby elastic
- One 3/4"-wide mother-of-pearl button
- Eight 2-1/4"-long spools of thread in your choice of colors
- 60-wt. ivory thread for embroidery
- Tear-away stabilizer
- Fiberfill
- Tapestry needle (size #18 or #22)
- Basic sewing supplies

Embroidery Designs

Martha Pullen's *Martha & Friends Series Vintage Baby, Disk 1* embroidery CD (design mpc1939)

Cutting

From candy pink silk dupioni, cut the following:

- one 8" square*
- one 6-1/2" square*

This project was designed using two 8" hemstitched linen napkins (blank linen area inside hemstitching, 5-3/4" square). Adjustments should be made to silk squares to accommodate other sized napkins. White linen napkins may be purchased and dyed using coffee or tea (see page 32).

Directions

Embellishment and Embroidery

1. Mark horizontal and vertical center of 8" square of candy pink silk with wash-away marker *(fig. 1)*.

2. Stabilize silk with tear-away stabilizer and triple straight stitch (L=4) along marked lines of 8" square of silk with 60-wt. ivory embroidery thread *(fig. 2)*. Remove stabilizer and press well.

3. Choose one of following methods for completing embroidery:

Stitch Designs Individually (4" x 4" hoop)

a. Print a template of embroidery design. Place template into each quadrant of silk and mark center for each design *(refer to fig. 2 for placement)*.

b. Hoop stabilizer and spray with temporary adhesive.

c. Center one quadrant of silk over stabilizer and embroider design according to embroidery machine manual *(see fig. 2)*. Rotate design as necessary.

d. Gently remove stabilizer.

e. Repeat steps b - d for remaining three quadrants until one embroidery design has been stitched in each corner of silk square *(see figure 2)*.

Combine Design in Embroidery Software (5" x 7" hoop)

a. Combine embroidery designs in computer software.

b. Hoop stabilizer and spray with temporary adhesive.

c. Center silk over stabilizer, using intersection of triple-stitched lines as design center. Embroider according to embroidery machine manual *(see fig. 2)*.

d. Gently remove stabilizer.

4. Press, embroidery side down, on a padded surface.

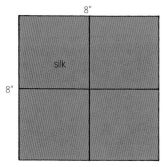

FIGURE 1

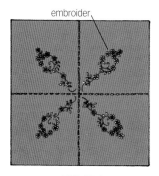

FIGURE 2

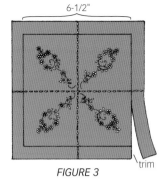

6-1/2"

trim

FIGURE 3

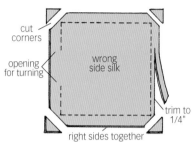

cut corners

opening for turning

wrong side silk

trim to 1/4"

right sides together

FIGURE 4

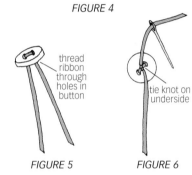

thread ribbon through holes in button

tie knot on underside

FIGURE 5   *FIGURE 6*

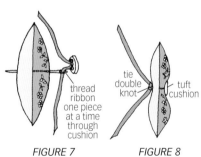

thread ribbon one piece at a time through cushion

tie double knot

tuft cushion

FIGURE 7   *FIGURE 8*

Construction

1. Measuring 3-1/4" from stitched vertical and horizontal center, mark a 6-1/2" square onto silk. Trim along marked lines *(fig. 3)*. Outermost edges of embroidery must be more than 1/2" from trimmed edge of 6-1/2" square.

2. Place 6-1/2" silk squares right sides together with raw edges even. Pin together and stitch with 1/2" seam allowance, leaving an opening for turning *(fig. 4)*.

3. Clip corners and trim seam allowance to 1/4" *(see fig. 4)*.

4. Turn square right side out, using a turner to push out side seams and corners. Press, embellished side down, on a padded surface.

5. Stuff pincushion firmly with polyester fiberfill and slip-stitch opening closed.

6. Cut 9" of sage green 1/8"-wide ribbon. Thread ribbon through holes in button *(fig. 5)* and tie a knot on underside of button *(fig. 6)*.

7. Thread large tapestry needle with one end of ribbon *(see fig. 6)*. Push needle through center front of pincushion to underside *(fig. 7)*. Remove ribbon end from needle and repeat for other ribbon end, entering close to but not in same hole as first ribbon. Tie ribbon ends in a double knot on back of pincushion, pulling tightly on button to tuft pincushion *(fig. 8)*.

8. Mark a miter line at each corner of one linen napkin (*fig. 9*).

9. Place napkins wrong sides together and pin, aligning hemstitching. Straight stitch (L=2.0-2.5) around napkins just inside hemstitching (*fig. 9*).

10. Stitch bar tacks (L=3.0-3.5) on outside center edges of each side and 1" from each corner (*see fig. 9*).

11. Thread bodkin with 1/8"-wide sage green ribbon. Beginning at one corner and leaving a 6" tail on underside, weave ribbon through hemstitching, over two threads, then under two threads (*fig. 10*). When ribbon has been woven around napkin, tie knot on underside and trim tails. Marked miter lines should be on top napkin.

12. Working on a lace shaping board, pin straight edge of ruffled ribbon to linen napkin just beyond outside edge of hemstitching. Miter corners and apply ribbon as follows:

a. Allow ribbon to extend past miter line. Place a pin at A and B along miter line. Fold ribbon back on itself, folding at B. Remove pin at A and reinsert pin through both layers of ribbon (*fig. 11*).

b. Continue pinning ribbon along outside edge of hemstitching (*fig. 12*). Miter remaining corners in same manner.

c. When you reach beginning of ribbon, overlap ribbons approximately 1". Trim away excess ribbon. Fold ribbon on top under 1/2" and pin in place (*fig. 13*).

d. Stitch inside edge of ribbon to napkin with narrow zigzag (L=2.0, W=2.0-2.5) (*fig. 14*).

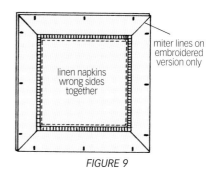

FIGURE 9

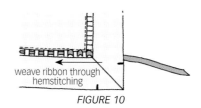

weave ribbon through hemstitching

FIGURE 10

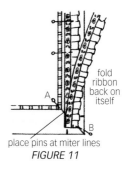

fold ribbon back on itself

place pins at miter lines

FIGURE 11

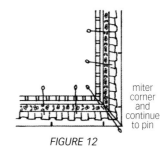

miter corner and continue to pin

FIGURE 12

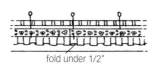

fold under 1/2"

FIGURE 13

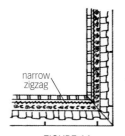

narrow zigzag

FIGURE 14

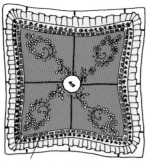

slip-stitch edge of silk pillow to napkins

FIGURE 15

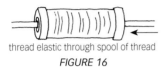

thread elastic through spool of thread

FIGURE 16

nestle spools between napkin layers
running elastic behind bartacks

FIGURE 17

13. Place pincushion right side up in center of embellished napkin. Pin pincushion seam line just inside napkin hemstitching. Slip stitch napkins to pincushion *(fig. 15)*.

14. Beginning at one corner and leaving a 6" tail of elastic, thread narrow elastic through holes of one spool of thread *(fig. 16)* and fit spool into pocket formed by bar tacks between napkins. Thread elastic behind bar tack and repeat with next thread spool *(fig. 17)*. When all spools have been inserted, tie elastic tails in a knot, tightening enough to hold spools snugly. Trim tails of elastic and tuck knot inside corner to hide from view.

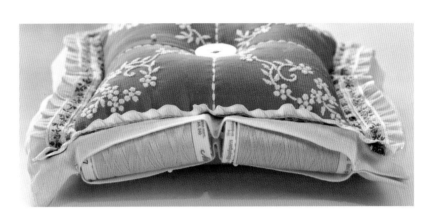

DYEING LACES AND FABRICS WITH COFFEE OR TEA

When only ecru will give your project the vintage effect you're after, coffee or tea will shade natural fiber fabrics and laces in lovely antique hues. The simple dyeing process can be repeated several times to deepen the color tone. A stronger brew of coffee or tea also darkens the stain. Just be sure to dye all materials for a project or ensemble at the same time to ensure color consistencies.

Supplies

- Fabric or lace to be dyed
- Water tight and color fast container for dye bath
- *2 cups strong coffee or tea
- *1/4 cup white vinegar

* Increase quantities in proportion to amount of lace or fabric you are dyeing. Liquid should completely cover lace or fabric.

A small sample should be tested before dyeing materials for your project. A coffee bath will result in subtle brown tones, and a tea bath will result in brown tones with a golden cast.

Dyeing Directions

1. Rinse lace or fabric with clear water, wetting lace or fabric thoroughly. Squeeze excess water from lace or fabric. Do not wring or twist lace or fabric. Set lace or fabric aside.

2. Stir together coffee/tea and vinegar in container.

3. Add wet lace or fabric to container, completely submerging lace or fabric into coffee or tea bath. Soak for 5 minutes up to several hours.

4. Remove from bath and rinse thoroughly in clear water.

5. Repeat process if lace or fabric is not dark enough, or increase strength of coffee or tea brewed.

6. Dry on a flat surface. Do not press lace or fabric until it is completely dry or it will streak.

7. When dry, press well to further set color.

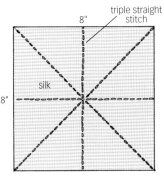

FIGURE a

For Pastel Version

1. Substitute 1/4 yard pink small gingham check silk dupioni for candy pink silk and omit ruffled miniature rose ribbon in supply list. Lightly coffee dye the silk to blend with the ecru napkins.

2. Omit *Embellishment and Embroidery* section.

3. On right side of 8" square of pink gingham check, mark horizontal, vertical and diagonal centers. Place tear-away stabilizer behind square and triple straight stitch (L=4) with 60-wt. ivory embroidery thread along each marked line. Remove stabilizer and press piece well *(fig. a)*.

4. Complete construction of pincushion, omitting step 12 (attaching ruffled ribbon).

Notions and Treasure Keeper

Every sewing room has its own assortment of small, useful tools and bits of fabric and lace left over from memorable projects: A few inches of ribbon from the roll used on a daygown, a package of needles or a tube of basting glue, a fabric marker and two snaps from a package of eight (you only needed six at the time). These are things that don't really belong anywhere in particular, but you know it's only a matter of time before you'll be looking for just that notion to put the finishing touch on some other project. Keep your little notion treasures in an elegant bowl-shaped notions keeper. Extra bobbins, measuring tape and a spare box of glass head pins – will always be handy in this lovely basket, tastefully coordinated with your fine sewing accessories ensemble and just the rainy day project you were looking for to use up those four extra mother-of-pearl buttons.

Supplies

- 1/2 yard silk dupioni (candy pink) for lining (Fabric 1)
- 1/2 yard silk jacquard (taupe) (Fabric 2)
- 1/2 yard Floriani Heat N Sta® fusible fleece
- 1 yard 1/4"-wide silk satin ribbon in your choice of color
- Four 3/4" mother-of-pearl buttons
- Basic sewing supplies

Cutting

From candy pink silk (Fabric 1) cut one 17" square

From taupe silk jacquard (Fabric 2) cut one 17" square

From fusible fleece cut one 17" square

Construction

1. Lightly fuse fleece square to wrong side of Fabric 1 square following manufacturer's directions *(fig. 1).*

2. Pin Fabric 1 square to Fabric 2 square, right sides together, matching raw edges. Straight stitch (L=2.0-2.5) through all layers with 1/2" seam allowance, leaving an opening for turning.

3. Trim corners. Pull batting away from fabric within seam allowance. Trim batting only very close to stitching *(fig. 2a).* Trim seam allowance of fabrics to 1/4" *(fig. 2b).* Serge or overcast seam allowances together.

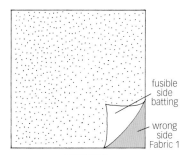

fusible side batting

wrong side Fabric 1

FIGURE 1

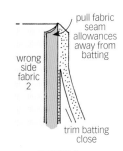

pull fabric seam allowances away from batting

wrong side fabric 2

trim batting close

FIGURE 2a

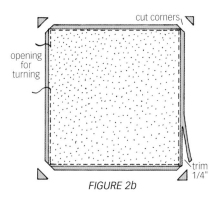

cut corners

opening for turning

trim 1/4"

FIGURE 2b

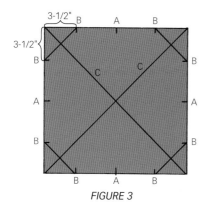

FIGURE 3

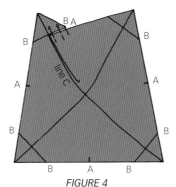

FIGURE 4

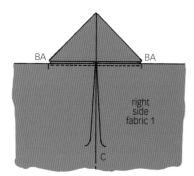

FIGURE 5

4. Turn square right side out through opening. Use point turner to gently push out corners and sides. Press well using a press cloth. Slip-stitch opening closed.

5. With chalk fabric marker, mark center of each side (A) *(fig. 3)*. Mark both fabric sides of piece.

6. On Fabric 1 side, place a mark 3-1/2" from each corner on all sides (B). Draw a line across each corner, connecting these marks.

7. On Fabric 1 side, draw a diagonal line from each corner to its opposite corner (C) *(fig. 3)*.

8. With Fabric 1 side facing out, pin point A to point B on one side having seamed edges even. Pin fold of fabric to inside at Line C, keeping seamed edges even with line drawn connecting points B *(fig. 4)*.

9. Repeat step 8 with adjacent side of corner *(fig. 5)*.

10. Repeat steps 8 and 9 for remaining corners.

11. With thread to match Fabric 1 in machine needle and thread to match fabric 2 in bobbin, straight stitch (L=2.0-2.5) across corner, catching folds in stitching *(fig. 5)*. This will be much easier to stitch if you remove machine tray and use free arm. Keeper will slip over end of free arm.

12. Turn keeper with Fabric 2 side out. Fold corners on B lines to outside and pin. Stitch one mother-of-pearl button to each corner, just above point *(see finished drawing)*.

13. Thread bodkin with silk satin ribbon. Guide ribbon under folded corners around top of notion keeper, leaving a 10" tail. Tie ribbon tails in a bow *(see finished drawing)*.

NOTIONS AND TREASURE KEEPER
FINISHED DRAWING

For Pastel Version:
Substitute the following in the supply list:
- 1/2 yard taupe/pink/ivory silk dupioni stripe (Fabric 1), for candy pink silk
- 1/2 yard natural linen blend (Fabric 2) for silk jacquard

Scissors Sleeve

Even a beginning seamstress soon learns the value of specialized scissors. She might easily use dressmaker's scissors, embroidery snips, and lace trimming scissors in the course of an hour's work! Of course, she wants the scissors collection out of the way of her project and yet readily accessible when the need for a specific pair arises. Here is the answer to her dilemma! A soft, silky sleeve to cushion and care for these all-important shears while keeping them handy for every need. This simple sheath starts as a rectangle but when folded by unique design, forms a sleek triangle with three handy scissors pockets. The discerning seamstress will hang this lovely holder near her sewing machine or cutting table and stock it with her trademark tools – her treasured scissors.

Supplies

- 3/8 yard silk dupioni (candy pink), 45" wide (Fabric 1)
- 1/3 yard silk dupioni (ecru), 45" wide (Fabric 2)
- One 10-1/2" x 12-1/2" rectangle Floriani Heat N Sta Fleece®
- 1/8 yard 1/8"-wide green silk satin ribbon
- Mettler® 60-wt. cotton thread (Color #512) for machine embroidery
- Lightweight tear-away stabilizer
- Basic sewing supplies

Cutting

All measurements are given width by length.

From candy pink silk dupioni (Fabric 1), cut one 10-1/2" x 12-1/2" rectangle

From ecru silk dupioni (Fabric 2), cut one 8-1/2" x 10-1/2" rectangle

Embroidery Design

Martha Pullen's *Martha & Friends Series Vintage Baby, Disk 1* embroidery CD (design mpc1901)

Templates

Folding Template (page 68)

Embroidery

1. Center and mark a rectangle 8-1/2"-wide x 10-1/2" long inside larger rectangle (Fabric 1) as shown *(fig. 1)*.

2. On right side of Fabric 1 rectangle, mark embroidery center 1-7/8" from right edge of **drawn rectangle** and 1-5/8" from bottom edge of **drawn rectangle** with wash-away marker as shown. Mark horizontal embroidery center with arrow toward seam allowance to indicate top of design *(fig. 1)*.

3. **Lightly** fuse fleece to wrong side of larger rectangle following manufacturer's instruction *(fig. 2)*.

4. Hoop tear-away stabilizer and mark stabilizer center.

5. Thread machine with embroidery thread in needle and bobbin.

6. Spray fleece side of Fabric 1 with temporary adhesive and center mark for embroidery onto stabilizer, fabric side up, making certain marked arrow is toward top of hoop.

7. Embroider design according to your embroidery machine manual directions.

8. Remove excess stabilizer from fleece/fabric unit. Trim away excess fleece and fabric outside drawn rectangle *(fig. 3)*.

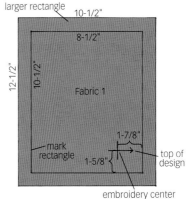

FIGURE 1

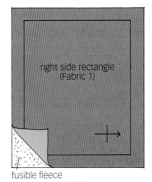

FIGURE 2

FIGURE 3

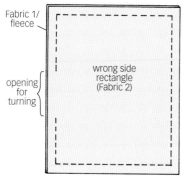

Fabric 1/ fleece

opening for turning

wrong side rectangle (Fabric 2)

FIGURE 4

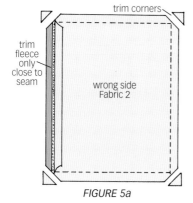

trim corners

trim fleece only close to seam

wrong side Fabric 2

FIGURE 5a

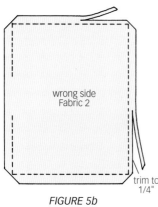

wrong side Fabric 2

trim to 1/4"

FIGURE 5b

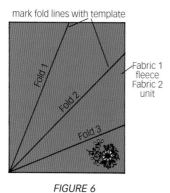

mark fold lines with template

Fold 1

Fold 2

Fold 3

Fabric 1 fleece Fabric 2 unit

FIGURE 6

Construction

1. Place Fabric 1/fleece and remaining fabric rectangle (Fabric 2) right sides together, matching raw edges. Pin in place. Straight stitch (L=2.0-2.5) around rectangle with 1/2" seam, leaving an opening for turning *(fig. 4)*.

2. Trim corners. Pull fleece away from fabric within seam allowance. Trim **fleece only** close to stitching *(fig. 5a)*. Trim fabric seam allowance to 1/4" *(fig. 5b)*. Serge or overcast seam allowances together.

3. Turn rectangle right side out through opening. Use point turner to gently push out corners and sides. Press well using press cloth. Slip-stitch opening closed.

4. Place piece on a flat surface with Fabric 1 facing up and embroidery in lower right corner.

5. Using the Folding Template as a guide, mark fold lines on embroidered side of piece with a chalk marker *(fig. 6)*.

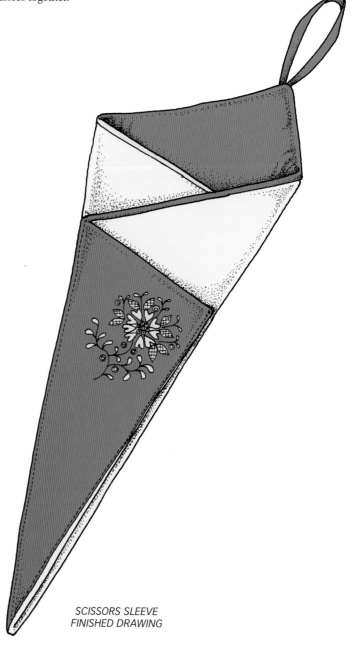

SCISSORS SLEEVE FINISHED DRAWING

6. Fold down upper left corner on Foldline 1, matching side of rectangle with Foldline 2 (*fig. 7*). Pin in place and press.

7. Next, fold bottom right corner (with embroidery) up, matching Foldline 3 with Foldline 1 as shown (*fig. 8*). Pin in place and press.

8. Fold corner (with embroidery) back, matching edge to Foldline 2.

The smallest section with embroidery will be on top (*fig. 9*). Pin in place and press using a press cloth.

9. Straight stitch (L=2.0 - 2.5) each side of top pocket through all layers to secure (*fig. 10*).

10. Fold silk ribbon in half forming a loop and stitch by hand to back of scissors sleeve for hanging (*see finished drawing*).

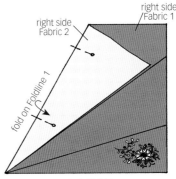

FIGURE 7

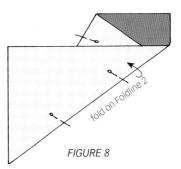

FIGURE 8

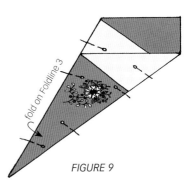

FIGURE 9

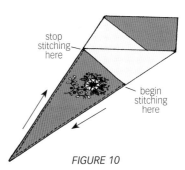

FIGURE 10

For Pastel Version:

Substitute the following in supply list:

- 3/8 yard linen blend (natural), 43/44" wide (Fabric 1), for candy pink silk dupioni
- 1/3 yard silk dupioni stripe (taupe/pink/ivory), 45" wide (Fabric 2) (stripes should run lengthwise - along 10-1/2" side), for ecru silk dupioni
- 1/8 yard of 1/8"-wide peach silk satin ribbon, for green silk satin ribbon

Elegant Sewing Organizer with Wrist Pincushion

Sew on the go in elegant heirloom style! This marvelous organizer showcases your handiwork and lets you take your projects anywhere in one package; it's as beautiful as it is convenient. The interior holds your threads, notions and small projects in pockets trimmed with decorative machine stitches: pinstitches, scallops, rows of bows and featherstitches. An eyelet border and hemstitching dress up linen pocket front, and breathtaking machine embroidery adorns the outside along with a contrasting silk ruffle and mother-of-pearl buttons strikingly similar to the embroidery pattern. The accompanying pincushion, with its ring of graceful silk petals, buttons to the front of the bag while a soft, comfortable wrist strap makes this sewing accessory a pleasure to take everywhere you go!

Please read through all directions before beginning.

Construction of pincushion included with this project was demonstrated on *Martha's Sewing Room*, Show #2601.

Supplies

- 7/8 yard silk dupioni (candy pink), 45" wide
- 3/4 yard linen blend (natural), 43/44" wide
- 1/3 yard pin wale piqué (brown) 60" wide
- 7/8 yard silk dupioni check (candy pink/brown) 45" wide
- 2/3 yard 5/8"-wide lace beading (ecru)
- 1-1/4 yards 1/4"-wide silk satin ribbon (ecru)
- Cotton thread for embroidery: Mettler® 60-wt. cotton (colors #512, ecru and #805, pink)
- Rayon thread for embroidery: Robison-Anton® 40-wt. rayon (colors #2567, mushroom; #2509, bitteroot; #2582, bone)
- Medium weight tear-away stabilizer for machine embroidery
- Lightweight tear-away stabilizer for decorative stitching
- Lightweight batting (12" x 21" rectangle and 7" square)
- 1/3 yard 1/4"-wide elastic for thread holder
- 1/4 yard 1/2"-wide elastic for wristband
- 5/8 yard gimp cord for gathering pincushion
- One 1/4" shank style pearl button (for seam ripper pocket)

- Two 5/8" shank style pearl buttons (for closure and for attaching pincushion)
- #100 wing needle or #100-#110 universal machine needle
- 60 or 80-wt. thread for wing-needle work (ecru)
- Circular attachment for machine (optional)
- Open-toe or clear machine foot
- Cording foot or pintuck foot for sewing machine
- Fiberfill
- Basic sewing supplies

Patterns and Templates

Large Inside Curved Pocket (page 65)

Small Inside Curved Pocket (page 66)

Seam Ripper Pocket (page 66)

Scissors Pocket (page 66)

Curved Embroidered Front (page 64)

Pincushion Front Circle (page 67)

Pincushion Back Circle (page 67)

Pincushion Petals (page 67)

Embroidery Designs

The Vintage Collection of Martha Pullen, Volume I, Disk 1 embroidery CD (designs mpc05020; mpc05021)

This Sewing Accessory book contains pictures of a bright version and a pastel version organizer. The bright version, shown below, is slightly smaller than the pastel version and has a different inside organizer and pocket layout.
NOTE: All templates, cutting instructions, and directions described within this book will create larger-sized organizer, which better accommodates embroidery and pocket layouts shown on inside of organizer.

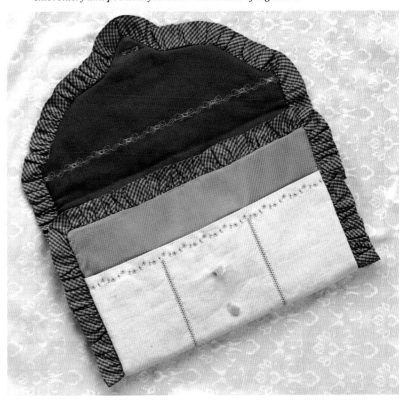

Cutting

Cut and label all pieces to avoid confusion during construction. The pieces listed below have a corresponding letter that will also be referenced during construction. Label each piece with a sticky dot and corresponding letter. All measurements are given width by length.

From candy pink silk dupioni, cut the following (refer to cutting guide, page 70):

- one 15" x 27" rectangle for organizer front (A)
- one 22" x 2-1/2" strip for strap (B)
- two 10" squares for large curved pocket (C)
- one 5" x 8" rectangle for small pocket (D)
- two 3" x 5" rectangles for scissors pocket (E)
- one 3" x 6" rectangle for seam ripper pocket (F)
- two 4" squares for pincushion back circle (G)
- one 2" x 16" bias strip for pincushion wristband (H)

From natural linen blend, cut the following (refer to cutting guide, page 71):

- one 4" square for embroidery appliqué (I)
- one 14" x 25" rectangle for organizer inside (J)
- one 14" x 10" rectangle for outside pocket (K)
- one 7" square for pincushion front circle (L)

From batting, cut the the following:

- one 14" x 25" rectangle (M)
- one 7" square for pincushion front circle (N)

From brown piqué, cut the following:

- one 14" x 18" rectangle for large end pocket (O)
- one 3" x 6" rectangle for seam ripper pocket lining (P)

From silk dupioni check, cut following (refer to cutting guide, page 71):

- one 20" x 3" strip for thread holder (Q)
- Five 3" x 30" bias strips for ruffle (R)
- Six 3-1/2" x 11" bias strips for pincushion petals (S)

Stabilizer will be cut as needed.

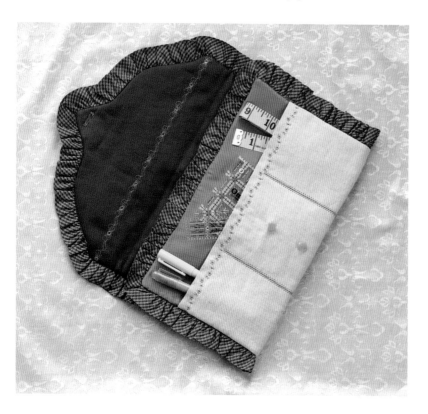

SEWING ORGANIZER

Creating Organizer Front (Outside)

Machine Cutwork/ Appliqué Embroidery Definitions

When doing machine embroidery cutwork/appliqué work, use detailed instructions described below for appropriate step named in a color sequence.

Appliqué Step #1 - Embroider a straight-stitch cutwork and placement line for appliqué. Remove hoop from machine. Trim inside cutwork line and remove fabric. Return hoop to machine. Place appliqué fabric over placement line.

Appliqué Step #2 - Embroider a zig-zag tackdown line on appliqué fabric. Remove hoop from machine. Trim and remove any excess appliqué fabric or threads outside tackdown line. Return hoop to machine.

Appliqué Step #3 - Embroider a satin stitch finished edge on appliqué fabric.

Embroidery

1. Fold 15" x 27" organizer front rectangle (A) to measure 7-1/2" x 27" and crease. Open piece and mark center line using a wash-out marker *(fig. 1)*. Locate 4" square of fabric (I) for embroidery appliqué.

2. Embroidery designs mpc05020 and mpc05021 were combined on organizer's front curved edge. Using embroidery software or your embroidery machine, place design mpc05020 in center and design mpc05021 on each side of center design, mirror imaging one side. Print out a template of de-

signs to help in placement. Refer to drawing for placement *(fig. 2)*.

3. Choose a hoop to fit combined design. Hoop a medium weight tear-away stabilizer. Fold and mark horizontal and vertical center on stabilizer using a wash-out marker. Using a printed template of combined embroidery design, place center mark of combined embroidery design on fabric center line 6" from one cut edge end of organizer front fabric *(see fig. 1)*. Spray stabilizer with a temporary adhesive spray and align fabric and stabilizer centers.

4. Wind a bobbin with 60-wt ecru cotton thread. Insert a wing needle or a large needle (#100-#110). Thread needle with 60-wt. Mettler® cotton thread #805 for first color in design.

5. Embroider design as follows:

Color 1 – Wing-needle work (60-wt. Mettler® #805) *after wing-needle work, remove wing-needle and replace with a #75 or #80 embroidery needle. Thread needle with Mettler® 60-wt. ecru cotton thread #512.*

Color 2 - Mettler® #512 - *Appliqué Step #1* for center design

Color 3 - Mettler® #512 - *Appliqué Step #2* for center design

Color 4 - Mettler® #512 - *Appliqué Step #3* and finish center embroidery

Color 5 - Mettler® #512 - *Appliqué Step #1* for side design

Color 6 - Mettler® #512 - *Appliqué Step #2* for side design

Color 7 - Mettler® #512 - *Appliqué Step #3* and finish side embroidery

Color 8, 9, & 10 - repeat color sequences 5, 6, & 7, respectively, for other side design

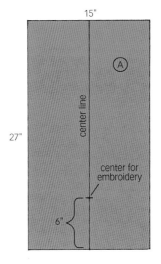

FIGURE 1

FIGURE 2

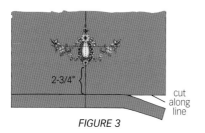

2-3/4"

cut along line

FIGURE 3

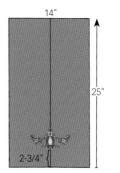

14"

25"

2-3/4"

FIGURE 4

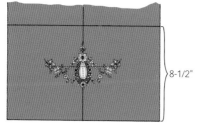

8-1/2"

FIGURE 5

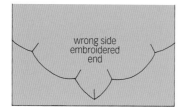

wrong side embroidered end

FIGURE 6

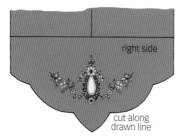

right side

cut along drawn line

FIGURE 7

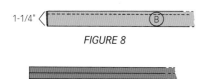

1-1/4"

B

FIGURE 8

FIGURE 9

6. When embroidery is complete, remove fabric from hoop and carefully trim away excess stabilizer and clip threads. Press embroidery from wrong side on a folded towel using a press cloth. Measure 2-3/4" from lowest edge of embroidery and mark. With a ruler, draw a horizontal line at mark, parallel to lower cut edge of rectangle. Cut along this line *(fig. 3)*. Do not trim additional fabric length from embroidered end of rectangle. Trim excess length from end opposite embroidery so height is 25". Keeping design centered horizontally, trim an equal vertical amount from each side so width is 14". This 14" x 25" embroidered rectangle now represents construction size for organizer front *(fig. 4)*.

7. On embroidered end of organizer front, draw a line across organizer 8-1/2" from raw edge of fabric. This line is for strap placement *(fig. 5)*. Using curved front paper template, trace cutting line and pivot lines with a wash-out marker onto wrong side of embroidered end of organizer front *(fig. 6)*. Cut organizer front along drawn cutting line *(fig. 7)*. Set piece aside.

Construction
Creating and Attaching Strap

1. Place an #80 universal needle in machine. This needle will be used for all construction and decorative machine embroidery unless a wing needle is designated.

2. Fold 22" x 2-1/2" strip for strap (B) in half, right sides together, to measure 22" x 1-1/4" and stitch long raw edges together using a 1/4" seam *(fig. 8)*. Turn right side out. Center seam in back and press *(fig. 9)*.

3. Cut a 24" strip of beading. Lightly starch and press beading without distorting shape. Center beading onto right side of strap. Stitch beading to strap with a narrow zigzag (L=2.0, W=1.5-2.0). Trim excess beading from each end of strap.

4. Weave a 26" long piece of 1/4"-wide ribbon through beading with a bodkin. Trim beading and ribbon even with ends of strap *(fig. 10).*

5. Pin strap to organizer front centered over strap placement line previously marked, matching ends of straps with each side of organizer front. There will be excess strap in center of organizer front to be used as a handle.

6. Stitch along one side fold of strap from outside cut edges of organizer to center of organizer front; turn and stitch across beading/ribbon; and turn back along other side of strap, ending at same side on which you started. Repeat for other side of strap. Where strap meets in center you should have about 8" unstitched that will form a 4" loop to carry organizer *(fig. 11).*

Outside Pocket

1. Fold 14" x 10" outside pocket rectangle (K) right sides together to measure 14" x 5". Stitch 14" edges together with a 1/4" seam *(fig. 12)*. Press seam

open. Turn right side out and press having seam centered *(fig. 13).*

2. Thread machine with Mettler 60-wt. thread, color #805, pink. Stitch a decorative daisy stitch using a wing-needle along one folded edge *(fig. 14).*

3. Pin embroidered edge 2-1/2" from raw edge of organizer front (opposite end from embroidery). Measure and mark vertical center of pocket panel with a wash-out marker.

4. To make divided pockets, draw lines 2-1/2" on each side of marked center of pocket panel with a wash-out marker.

5. Stitch along two marked lines (not center line) with a wing needle and a decorative stitch such as daisy stitch, entredeux stitch or another stitch of your choice.

6. Change to a size #70 or #80 needle and stitch a decorative stitch such as a pinstitch or blanket stitch along bottom edge of pocket *(fig. 15).*

beading strip

zigzag edges to strap

FIGURE 10

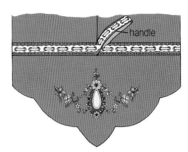

handle

FIGURE 11

14"

K

5"

FIGURE 12

FIGURE 13

daisy stitch

FIGURE 14

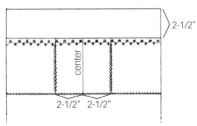

2-1/2"

center

2-1/2" 2-1/2"

FIGURE 15

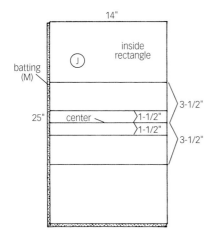

FIGURE 16

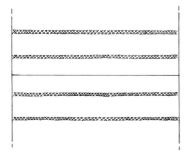

FIGURE 17

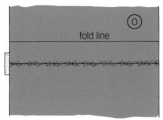

FIGURE 18a

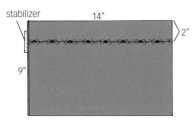

FIGURE 18b

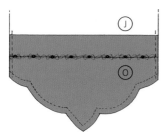

FIGURE 19

Creating Organizer Back (Inside)

1. Fold 14" x 25" organizer inside rectangle (J) in half to measure 14" x 12-1/2". Crease. Unfold and mark horizontal center across piece with a wash-out marker. This will be placement line for thread holder.

2. Measuring from center line, draw two more lines above and below center line at 1-1/2" and 3-1/2".

3. Spray 14" x 25" rectangle of batting (M) with temporary adhesive spray. Place wrong side of fabric rectangle on top of batting aligning raw edges *(fig. 16)*. Thread machine with Robison-Anton® #2567, mushroom. Select a decorative stitch such as a feather-stitch or another stitch of your choice. Sew decorative stitch along top two lines and bottom two lines to "quilt" organizer back to batting. ***NOTE:** A walking foot may be used (fig. 17).*

Large End Pocket

1. Fold 14" x 18" large end pocket rectangle (O) in half, wrong sides together, to measure 14" x 9". Press.

2. Draw a line across 14" width 2" from fold. Select a decorative machine stitch such as a bow design. Open rectangle and place a strip of lightweight tear-away stabilizer behind drawn line. Stitch design, using Robison-Anton® #2509, bitteroot *(fig. 18a)*. Remove stabilizer.

3. Fold fabric in half again and place a piece of lightweight tear-away stabilizer underneath. Select an eyelet stitch on your machine. Sew eyelet in center of bows through both layers. Use Fray Block™ on eyelets and then cut out centers with tiny pointed embroidery scissors *(fig. 18b)*. Remove stabilizer.

4. Pin pocket to organizer back, raw edges even. Trace cutting line from front template onto pocket. Cut organizer back/pocket along cutting line.

5. Baste along sewing line (1/2" seam allowance) on trimmed edge. This will give a line to follow when attaching organizer front and back *(fig. 19)*. Baste along sides of pocket/organizer with a 3/8" seam.

Thread Holder

1. Fold 20" x 3" thread holder strip (Q) in half, right sides together, to measure 20" x 1-1/2". Straight stitch long raw edges with a 1/2" seam allowance. Trim seam allowance to 1/4" *(fig. 20)* and press seam open.

2. Turn strip right side out placing seam in middle of strip and press *(fig. 21)*.

3. Straight stitch 1/4" away from each folded edge using Mettler® 60-wt. cotton #512, ecru. Mark vertical center of strip *(fig. 22)*.

4. Mark center line of organizer back every 1-1/2", measuring from vertical center to each end *(fig. 23)*. Insert a 14" piece of 1/4" elastic into casing strip and stitch across each end. With both hands, pull casing, stretching it out to distribute gathers evenly.

5. Stitch casing strip to organizer back at each side using a 1/2" seam allowance.

6. Pin strip to marks on organizer back aligning center mark on strip with center mark on organizer back.

7. Align and pin strip to 1-1/2" marks on organizer back. Stitch through both strip and organizer back with a zigzag stitch or narrow satin stitch *(fig. 24)*.

Large Curved Pocket

1. Place two 10" squares for large curved pocket (C) right sides together. Cut two large curved pockets from squares *(fig. 25)*.

2. Stitch pocket right sides together using a 1/2" seam allowance along stitching line marked on pattern piece *(fig. 26)*. Trim seam allowances to 1/4". Clip curves and corners *(fig. 27)*. Turn right side out and press *(fig. 28)*. Set pocket aside.

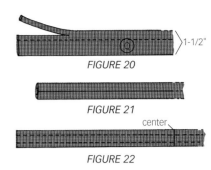

1-1/2"

FIGURE 20

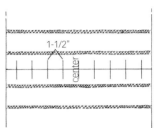

FIGURE 21

center

FIGURE 22

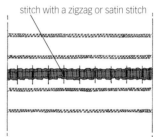

1-1/2"

center

FIGURE 23

stitch with a zigzag or satin stitch

FIGURE 24

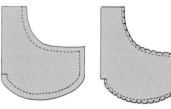

C

FIGURE 25

FIGURE 26   FIGURE 27

FIGURE 28

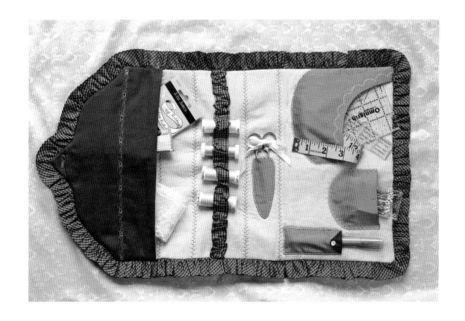

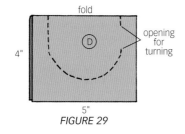

FIGURE 29

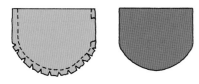

FIGURE 30   FIGURE 31

FIGURE 32   FIGURE 33

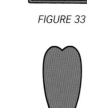

FIGURE 34   FIGURE 35

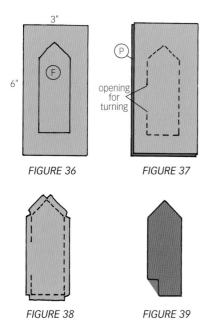

FIGURE 36   FIGURE 37

FIGURE 38   FIGURE 39

Small Curved Pocket

1. Fold 5" x 8" small pocket rectangle (D) in half, right sides together, to measure 5" x 4". Finger press.

2. Place top edge of pattern along fold of fabric. Trace stitching line from pattern onto fabric.

3. Straight stitch along drawn line leaving a small opening along one straight side for turning *(fig. 29)*. Cut out pocket 1/4" outside stitching line. Clip curves and corners *(fig. 30)*.

4. Turn pocket right side out through opening. Using a point turner, smooth seams. Turn 1/4" of both layers to inside at opening. Press well *(fig. 31)*. Set pocket aside. Opening will be stitched closed when pocket is attached to organizer.

Scissors Pocket

1. Trace stitching line from pattern onto wrong side of one 3" x 5" scissors pocket rectangle (E) *(fig. 32)*.

2. Place 3" x 5" pocket rectangles right sides together. Straight stitch along drawn line, leaving a small opening along one side for turning *(fig. 33)*.

Cut out pocket 1/4" outside stitching line. Clip curves and corners *(fig. 34)*.

3. Turn pocket right side out through opening. Using a point turner, smooth seams. Turn 1/4" of both layers to inside at opening. Press well. Set pocket aside *(fig. 35)*. Opening will be stitched closed when pocket is attached to organizer.

Seam Ripper Pocket

1. Trace stitching line from pattern onto wrong side of 3" x 6" seam ripper pocket rectangle (F) *(fig. 36)*.

2. Place pocket rectangle and 3" x 6" seam ripper pocket lining rectangle (P) right sides together. Straight stitch along drawn line, leaving a small opening along one side for turning *(fig. 37)*. Cut out pocket 1/4" outside stitching line. Clip corners *(fig. 38)*.

3. Turn pocket right side out through opening. Using a point turner, smooth seams. Turn 1/4" of both layers to inside at opening. Press well *(fig. 39)*. Set pocket aside. Opening will be stitched closed when pocket is attached to organizer.

Embellishing and Attaching Inside Pockets

Pockets are attached with a blanket stitch, pinstitch or another decorative stitch of your choice.

1. Thread machine needle with Robison-Anton® #2582, bone and lightweight thread in bobbin.

2. Place lightweight stabilizer beneath large curved pocket. Select a decorative stitch such as a scallop stitch and sew along top finished curved edge *(fig. 40)*.

3. Place organizer back on a flat surface.

4. Position four created pockets onto piece as desired *(see figure 47 for suggested placement)*. Pin pockets in place. Lining side of seam ripper pocket will be toward organizer back. Mark ribbon position approximately 1" above scissor pocket. Placement will depend on size of scissors. When scissors are placed in pocket, tie a bow through handles to keep scissors from slipping out of pocket. Refer to *figure 41* for stitching all pockets.

5. Stitch scissors pocket in place with a pinstitch or blanket stitch starting and stopping at dots on pattern.

6. Stitch seam ripper pocket on three sides with a pinstitch or blanket stitch starting and stopping at foldline. Leave

pointed end open. Fold flap down over pocket and stitch in place with a small pearl button. Do not stitch pocket closed at top when attaching button.

7. Stitch small curved pocket in place with a decorative stitch, leaving top open.

8. Stitch large curved pocket in place with a decorative stitch. With a straight stitch, baste pocket to organizer along top and side.

9. Optional: Stitch a decorative stitch along designated line on pocket. This will create a division in pocket creating another small pocket for holding narrow items.

10. Cut a 12" piece of 1/4" ribbon. Fold ribbon in half and crease. Unfold and straight stitch ribbon to organizer back at mark above scissors pocket. Tie bow.

Completing Organizer

1. Using 1/4" seams, stitch all 3" x 30" ruffle strips (R), right sides together, creating one continuous strip *(fig. 42)*. Press seams open *(fig. 43)*.

2. Fold each short end of strip 1/2" to wrong side and press. Fold strip in half lengthwise, wrong sides together, and press. Stitch two rows of lengthened straight stitching at 3/8" and 5/8" from raw edge *(fig. 44)*.

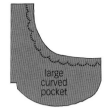

FIGURE 40

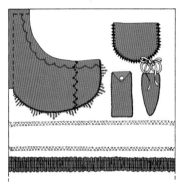

FIGURE 41

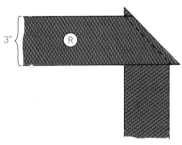

FIGURE 42

FIGURE 43

FIGURE 44

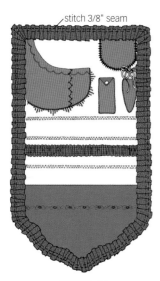

stitch 3/8" seam

FIGURE 45

wrong side organizer front

opening for turning

pivot lines

FIGURE 46

FIGURE 47

3. Pull up gathers on ruffle strip to fit outside edge of organizer back (inside). Pin ruffle to organizer, matching raw edges and adjusting ruffles as needed allowing extra fullness at corners.

4. Straight stitch ruffle to organizer back with a 3/8" seam *(fig. 45)*.

5. Pin organizer front and back right sides together sandwiching ruffle between.

6. Stitching from wrong side of organizer front, stitch layers together with a 1/2" seam, pivoting at designated marks (see *Curved Embroidery Front Template*). Leave 3" - 4" open at one side for turning *(fig. 46)*.

7. Clip curves, corners and pivot marks. Turn and press.

8. Stitch opening closed by hand *(fig. 47)*. Remove visible garing thread.

9. Stitch a 3/4" horizontal buttonhole at center front of organizer below embroidery.

10. Fold organizer *(refer to finished drawing)*. Sew a shank-style button to outside pocket underneath buttonhole *(see finished drawing)*.

11. Optional: Sew a second button 1-1/2" below first button to attach pincushion.

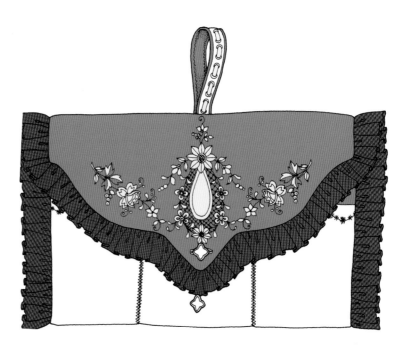

*ELEGANT ORGANIZER
FINISHED DRAWING*

WRIST PINCUSHION

Center Embroidery

1. Fold 7" square for pincushion front circle (L) in half vertically and horizontally. Crease and mark center of fabric with a wash-out marker *(fig. 1)*. Using Pincushion Front Circle Template trace outermost circle onto square *(fig. 2)*.

2. Thread machine needle with Robison-Anton® #2509 bitteroot and bobbin with lightweight thread.

3. Cut a 7" square of stabilizer.

4. If your sewing machine does not have a circular attachment, proceed to step 5. If your machine has a circular attachment, follow directions below:

a. Attach circular attachment to sewing machine following your machine's directions.

b. Layer 7" squares of stabilizer, batting (N) and fabric (L), right side up. Temporary spray adhesive may be used to adhere layers together.

c. Set circumference of circle at 2-1/4" (1-1/8" from needle to pin of attachment).

d. Place marked center of fabric onto pin of attachment and replace plastic cover if applicable. Using an open-toe or clear foot, sew a daisy stitch or other decorative stitch of your choice in a circle *(fig. 3)*.

5. If your machine does not have a circular attachment, follow directions below:

a. Center and trace small circle (decorative stitching line) from pincushion front circle template onto 7" fabric square.

b. Layer 7" squares of stabilizer, batting and fabric (right side up). Temporary spray adhesive may be used to adhere layers together.

c. Using an open-toe or clear foot, sew a daisy stitch or other decorative stitch of your choice along designated line pivoting often with needle down *(fig. 4)*.

6. Remove stabilizer *(fig. 5)*. Set square aside.

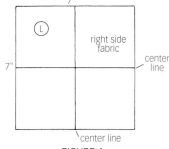

FIGURE 1

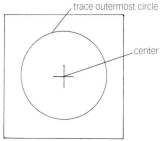

trace outermost circle

center

FIGURE 2

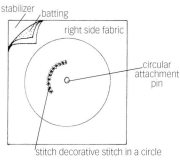

stabilizer
batting
right side fabric
circular attachment pin
stitch decorative stitch in a circle

FIGURE 3

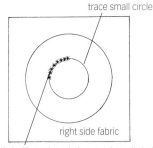

trace small circle

right side fabric

stitch decorative stitch around small circle

FIGURE 4

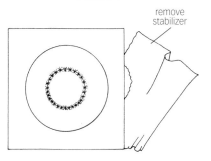

remove stabilizer

FIGURE 5

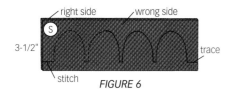

FIGURE 6

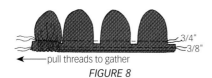

FIGURE 7

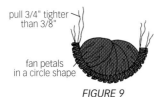

FIGURE 8

FIGURE 9

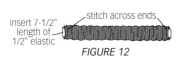

FIGURE 10   FIGURE 11

FIGURE 12

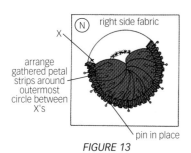

FIGURE 13

Creating Petals

1. Thread machine with thread to match pincushion petal fabric. Trace Petal Template onto wrong side of three of 3-1/2" x 11" bias strips (S).

2. Place one traced bias strip and one un-traced bias strip right sides together. Straight stitch along traced stitching line *(fig. 6)*.

3. Trim seam allowance to 1/4" (1/8" between petals). Clip curves and seam allowance between petals *(fig. 7)*.

4. Turn petals to right side and press.

5. Repeat steps 2 - 4 to create two more petal strips.

6. Stitch two rows of lengthened machine stitches at 3/8" and 3/4" along long raw edges of each strip. Each petal strip will be gathered individually.

7. Pull threads to gather petal strips *(fig. 8)*. Fan petals in a circle shape pulling 3/8" gathering stitch tighter than 3/4" gathering stitch *(fig. 9)*. Set pieces aside.

Creating Wristband

1. Fold 2" x 16" wristband bias strip (H) in half to measure 1" x 16", right sides together, and stitch with a 1/4" seam *(fig. 10)*. Turn and press strip aligning seam in center of strip *(fig. 11)*.

2. Cut a 7-1/2" length of 1/2"-wide elastic (adjust length to wrist measurement). Insert elastic with a bodkin into created casing and stitch across ends to secure elastic in casing *(fig. 12)*.

3. Set wristband aside.

Attaching Petals, Loop and Wristband

1. Arrange gathered petal strips around inside of outermost circle on linen square matching long straight edge of petal strip to outermost line. One gathered strip will be placed between X's designated on template. When adding another strip, overlap ends of strips so petals are touching or overlapping slightly. Pin petals in place *(fig. 13)*.

2. Straight stitch petals to linen square 1/2" from outermost circle *(fig. 14)*.

3. Press area between stitching and outermost drawn circle to flatten gathers in seam allowance *(see fig. 14)*.

4. Cut a 2-1/2" length of 1/4" ribbon. Fold in half creating a 1-1/4" loop *(fig. 15)*. Place folded loop behind one petal matching raw ends of ribbon to outermost circle. Machine stitch loop in place along previous stitching. For added security, stitch again just outside seam allowance 1/8" from first stitching *(fig. 16)*.

5. Pin wristband on top of petals with seam side of wristband facing you. Match ends of wristband to outermost circle and stitch along previous stitching line *(fig. 17)*. For added security, stitch again 1/8" from first stitching. Trim wristband close to second stitching *(see fig. 17)*.

Finishing Pincushion

1. Using a cording foot or pintuck foot to keep gimp cord centered, zigzag (L-2.0-2.5; W=3.0-4.0) over gimp cord (leaving a 4" - 5" tail) approximately 3/8" from outermost circle *(fig. 18)*. Continue around circle stopping where gimp began. Do not stitch through gimp cord.

2. Trim fabric/batting square along outermost drawn circle *(fig. 19)*. Do not cut gimp cord tails.

3. Pull gimp cord tails to gather tightly and tie off with a square knot.

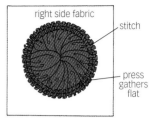

FIGURE 14

FIGURE 15

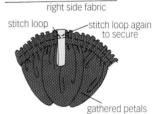

FIGURE 16

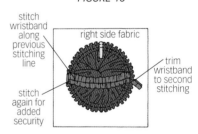

FIGURE 17

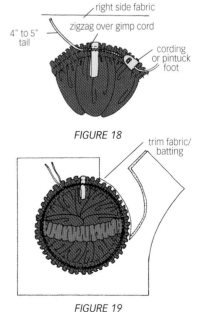

FIGURE 18

FIGURE 19

pull gimp cord
tails together
tightly and
tie off

FIGURE 20

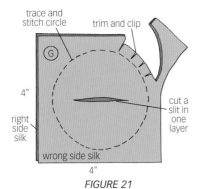

trace and
stitch circle

trim and clip

G

4"

right
side
silk

cut a
slit in
one
layer

wrong side silk

4"

FIGURE 21

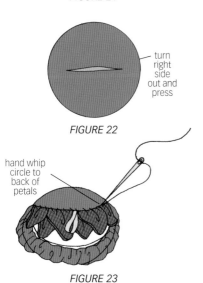

turn
right
side
out and
press

FIGURE 22

hand whip
circle to
back of
petals

FIGURE 23

4. With fiberfill, stuff pincushion tightly through opening *(fig. 20)*. An eraser end of a pencil may be used to push fiberfill into opening and fill void.

5. Create back circle for pincushion either by using your machine's circular attachment (pin will be placed 1-1/2" from needle) or trace Back Circle Template onto wrong side of one 4" pincushion back square (G).

6. Stitch two squares together along circle *(fig. 21)*.

7. Trim circle's seam allowance to 1/4". Clip seam allowance every 1/8"-1/4". Cut a slit in one layer of pink silk *(see fig. 21)*.

8. Turn circle right side out through opening and use a point turner to smooth circle. Press circle well *(fig. 22)*.

9. Flip wristband to front of pincushion so it is out of the way.

10. Center pincushion back circle, slit side against pincushion, and hand whip circle with matching thread to back of petals *(fig. 23)*.

11. Flip wristband to back of pincushion and "cup" petals around center *(see finished drawing)*.

12. For carrying, pincushion may be attached to organizer by ribbon loop over button on front of organizer.

*WRIST PINCUSHION
FINISHED DRAWING*

1. Substitute the following in the supply list:

- 7/8 yard of linen blend (natural) for candy pink silk dupioni
- 3/4 yard of linen blend (pink) for linen blend (natural)
- 3/4 yard of silk dupioni stripe (taupe/pink/ivory) for candy pink/brown silk dupioni
- 1-1/4 yards of 1/4"-wide peach silk satin ribbon for ecru ribbon

2. Omit brown pin wale piqué from supply list.

3. Add 1/8 yard pink silk organza to supply list.

4. From natural linen blend, cut pieces A, B, C, E, F, L, O and Q (refer to cutting guide).

5. From pink linen blend cut pieces J, K and G.

6. From pink silk organza, cut pieces D and I.

7. From taupe/pink/ivory silk dupioni stripe, cut pieces R, S, H and P

8. From batting, cut pieces M and N.

9. Use the following colors for embroidery and decorative stitching:

- Mettler® 60-wt. cotton thread for wing-needle work (color #512 ecru)
- Sulky® 40-wt. rayon thread (colors #1543 peach fluff and #1258 coral reef) for machine embroidery
- Sulky® 40-wt. rayon thread (color #1128, dark ecru) for decorative stitching

10. Use the following color sequence for organizer front embroidery:

Color 1 – Wing-needle work (Mettler 60-wt. thread, color #512 ecru) after wing-needle work, remove wing-needle and replace with a #75 or #80 embroidery needle.

Color 2 - Sulky® #1543 - *Appliqué Step #1* for center design

Color 3 - Sulky® #1543 - *Appliqué Step #2* for center design

Color 4 - Sulky® #1543 - *Appliqué Step #3* and finish center embroidery

Color 5 - Sulky® #1258 - *Appliqué Step #1* for side design

Color 6 - Sulky® #1258 - *Appliqué Step #2* for side design

Color 7 - Sulky® #1258 - *Appliqué Step #3* and finish side embroidery

Color 8, 9, & 10 - repeat color sequences 5, 6, & 7, respectively, for other side design

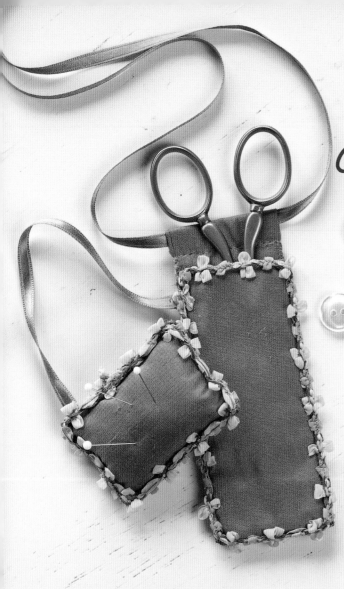

Chatelaine & Pincushion

We all know nothing slows sewing progress more than a need to search for scissors or a pin every time you want to snip a thread or hold a seam in place. Tools at hand, however, keep projects moving along. This simple one-hour project will immeasurably enhance efficiency of your sewing room. Quick to make and lovely to the eye and touch, this silk chatelaine and pincushion keep your most essential tools accessible. No more endless searching for those tiny snipping scissors – you'll find them in a pretty little silk pocket around your neck. Need a pin or two quickly? You won't even have to glance away from your work to snatch one! Make this set for yourself – and make one for a friend!

Please read through all directions before beginning.

Construction of this project was demonstrated on *Martha's Sewing Room*, Show #3107.

Supplies

- 1/8 yard silk dupioni (candy pink)
- One yard 1/8"-wide silk satin ribbon (moss)
- 2/3 yard decorative ribbon trim
- Polyester fiberfill
- Low loft batting
- Basic sewing supplies

Cutting

All measurements are given width by length.

From silk dupioni, cut the following:

- Two pieces 16" x 2-1/4"
- Two pieces 5" x 2-1/4"

From 1/8"-wide silk satin ribbon, cut the following:

- One piece 30" long
- One piece 6" long

From low loft batting, cut one piece 3-1/2" x 1-1/2"

Scissors Holder

1. Place 16" x 2-1/4" strips right sides together. Straight stitch both long sides with a 1/4" seam *(fig. 1)*.

2. Turn tube right side out and press well with long seams at each side *(fig. 2)*. This strip will now be treated and referenced as ribbon during construction.

3. Fold ribbon in half, right sides together, having cut edges even. Stitch across ends with a 1/4" seam *(fig. 3)*. Press seam open.

4. Turn ribbon right side out. Center seam on one side of ribbon and press ribbon flat.

5. Stitch across one end of folded ribbon 1/4" from fold to form casing for neck ribbon *(fig. 4)*. Thread to match ribbon or invisible thread may be used.

6. Slip batting piece between ribbons at casing end *(fig. 5)*.

7. Fold opposite end of ribbon up 3-1/2". Fold should fall just short of centered seam and end of batting. Pin side edges together and even *(fig. 6)*.

8. Place one end of 6" length of 1/8"-wide silk satin ribbon between edges of folded embroidered ribbon just below top of folded pocket. Insert enough ribbon to catch edge securely. Pin in place *(see fig. 7)*.

9. Zigzag along outside edges of ribbon pocket from bottom fold to – but not through – casing on both sides, catching end of 1/8"-wide ribbon in stitching on one side. Stitch with thread color matching ribbon or use invisible thread and a narrow zigzag (L=2.0; W=2.0-2.5). One swing of needle should land in ribbon while other swing should fall off edge, closing sides *(see figure 7)*.

10. Using a bodkin, thread one end of 30"-long piece of 1/8"-wide ribbon through casing. Tie ribbon ends together securely to knot. Slide ribbon so knot disappears into casing *(see finished drawing)*.

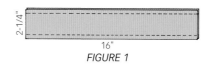

2-1/4" 16"

FIGURE 1

1-3/4" right side 16"

FIGURE 2

fold wrong side 1/4"

FIGURE 3

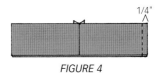

1/4"

FIGURE 4

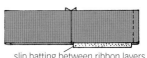

slip batting between ribbon layers

FIGURE 5

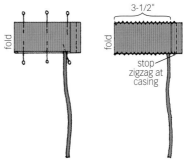

fold fold 3-1/2" stop zigzag at casing

FIGURE 6   *FIGURE 7*

*CHATELAINE AND PINCUSHION
FINISHED DRAWING*

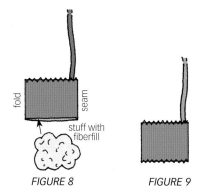

fold

seam

stuff with fiberfill

FIGURE 8   FIGURE 9

Pincushion

1. Place 5" x 2-1/4" strips right sides together. Straight stitch both long sides with a 1/4" seam (refer to fig. 1).

2. Turn tube right side out and press well with long seams at each side (refer to fig. 2). This strip will now be treated and referenced as ribbon during construction.

3. Fold 5" length of ribbon in half, right sides together, raw ends matching. Straight stitch with a 1/4" seam allowance (refer to figure 3).

4. Press seam open. Turn ribbon to right side keeping seam at one end.

5. Place free end of 6" length of ribbon attached to scissors pocket into one side of pincushion. Pin in place.

Zigzag (L=2.0; W=2.0-2.5) ribbon edge together along side with narrow ribbon (fig. 8).

6. Place a small amount of polyester fiberfill inside pincushion through open side (see fig. 8). Pin side edges together and zigzag side closed (L=2.0; W=2.0-2.5) (fig. 9).

Finishing

1. Hand stitch ribbon trim around outside edges of scissor pocket and pincushion using matching thread or invisible thread (see finished drawing for positioning trim).

2. Insert small scissors into pocket and pins and/or needles in pincushion.

For Pastel Version:

Substitute 2/3 yard 1-3/4"-wide floral embroidered ribbon (pink and green on light tan) for candy pink silk

From floral embroidered ribbon, cut the following:
- One piece 16" long
- One piece 5" long

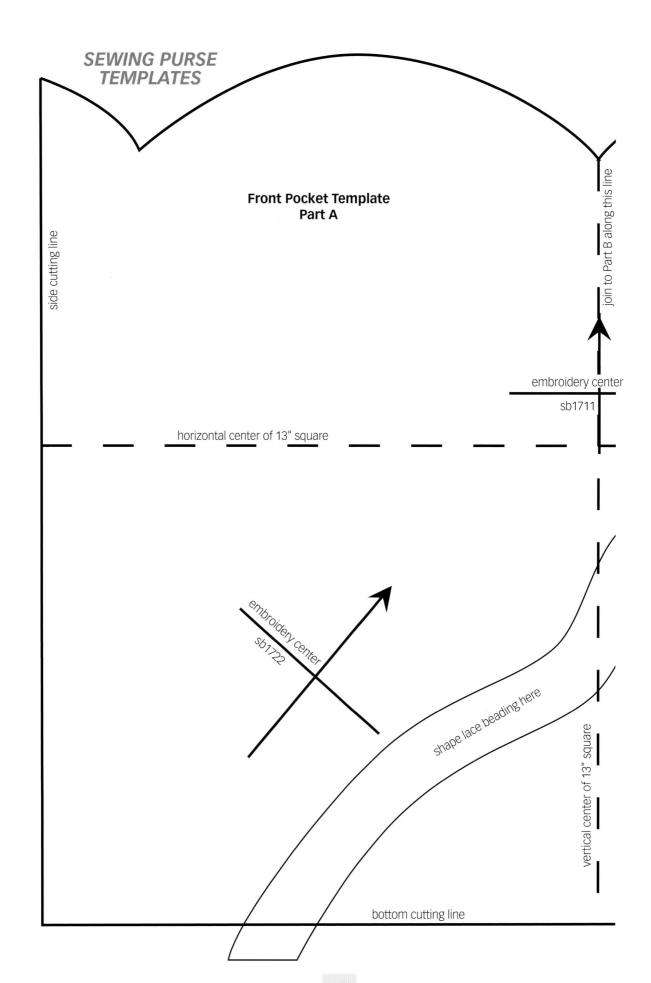

SEWING PURSE
TEMPLATES

**Front Pocket Template
Part A**

side cutting line

join to Part B along this line

embroidery center
sb1711

horizontal center of 13" square

embroidery center
sb1722

shape lace beading here

vertical center of 13" square

bottom cutting line

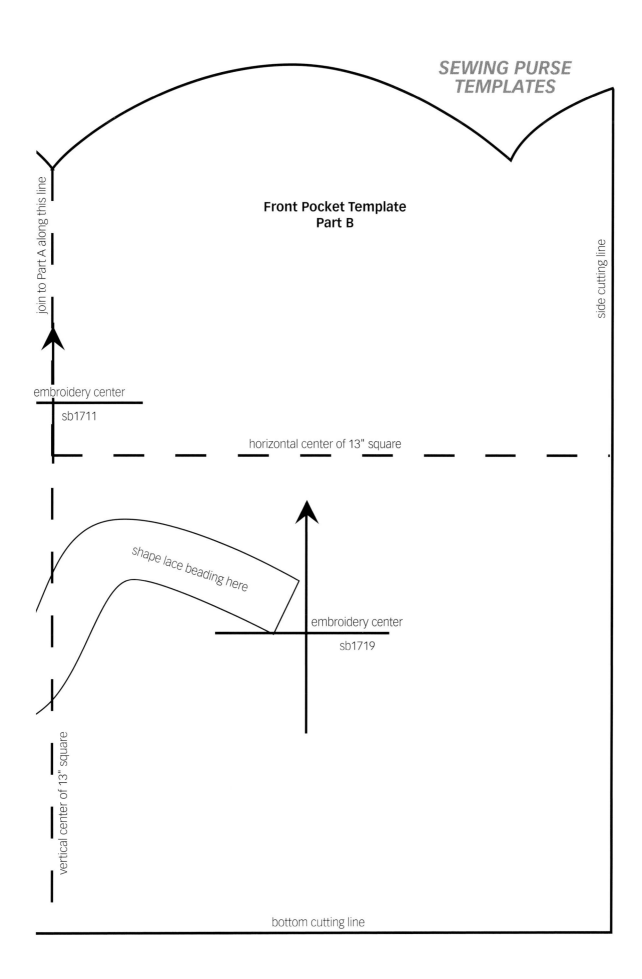

Front Pocket Template
Part B

join to Part A along this line

side cutting line

embroidery center

sb1711

horizontal center of 13" square

shape lace beading here

embroidery center

sb1719

vertical center of 13" square

bottom cutting line

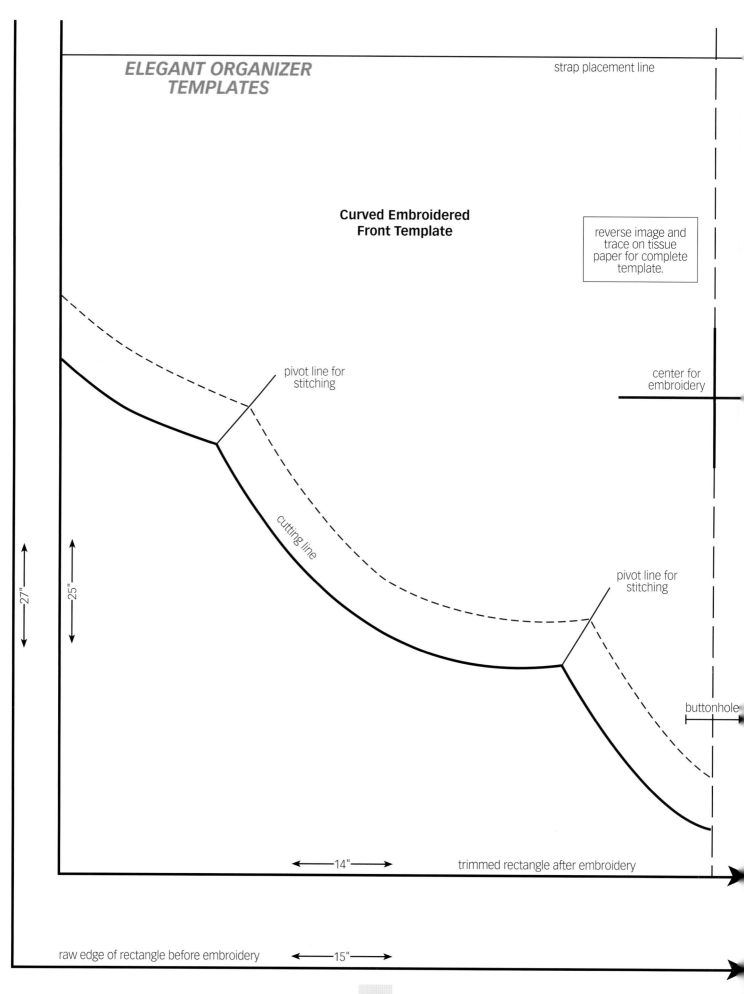

ELEGANT ORGANIZER
TEMPLATES

strap placement line

Curved Embroidered
Front Template

reverse image and
trace on tissue
paper for complete
template.

center for
embroidery

pivot line for
stitching

cutting line

pivot line for
stitching

buttonhole

27"

25"

14"

trimmed rectangle after embroidery

raw edge of rectangle before embroidery

15"

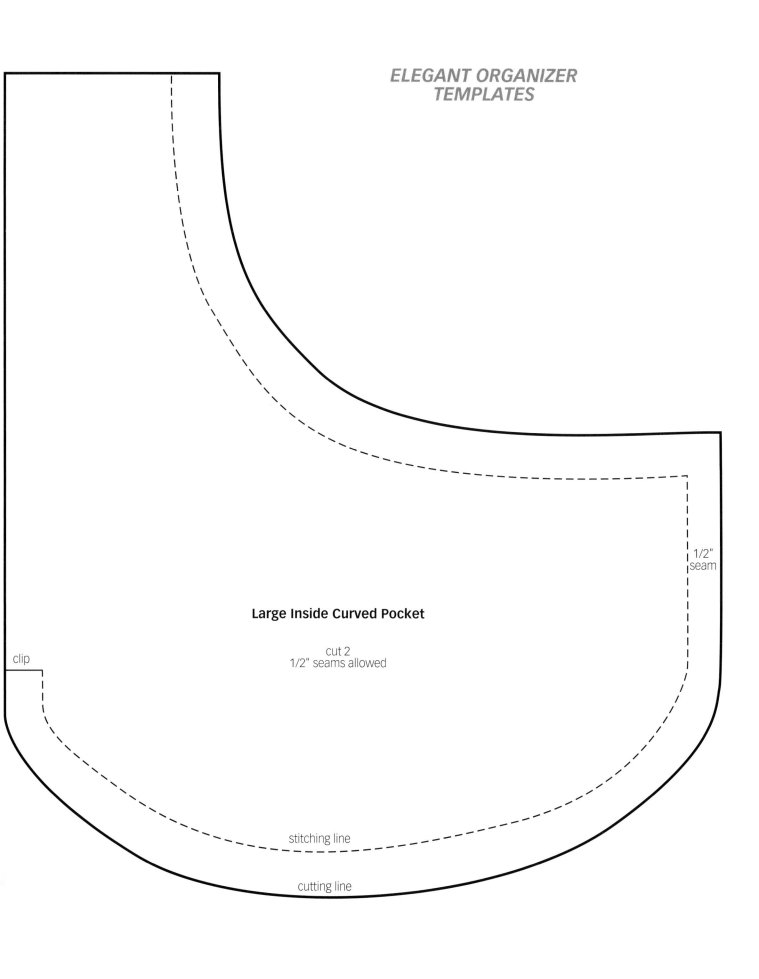

Large Inside Curved Pocket

cut 2
1/2" seams allowed

1/2"
seam

clip

stitching line

cutting line

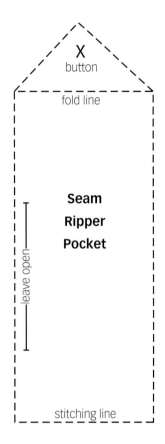

X
button

fold line

Seam

Ripper

Pocket

leave open

stitching line

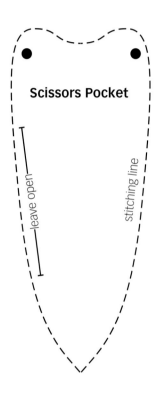

Scissors Pocket

leave open

stitching line

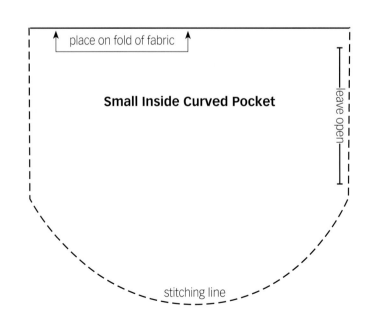

place on fold of fabric

Small Inside Curved Pocket

leave open

stitching line

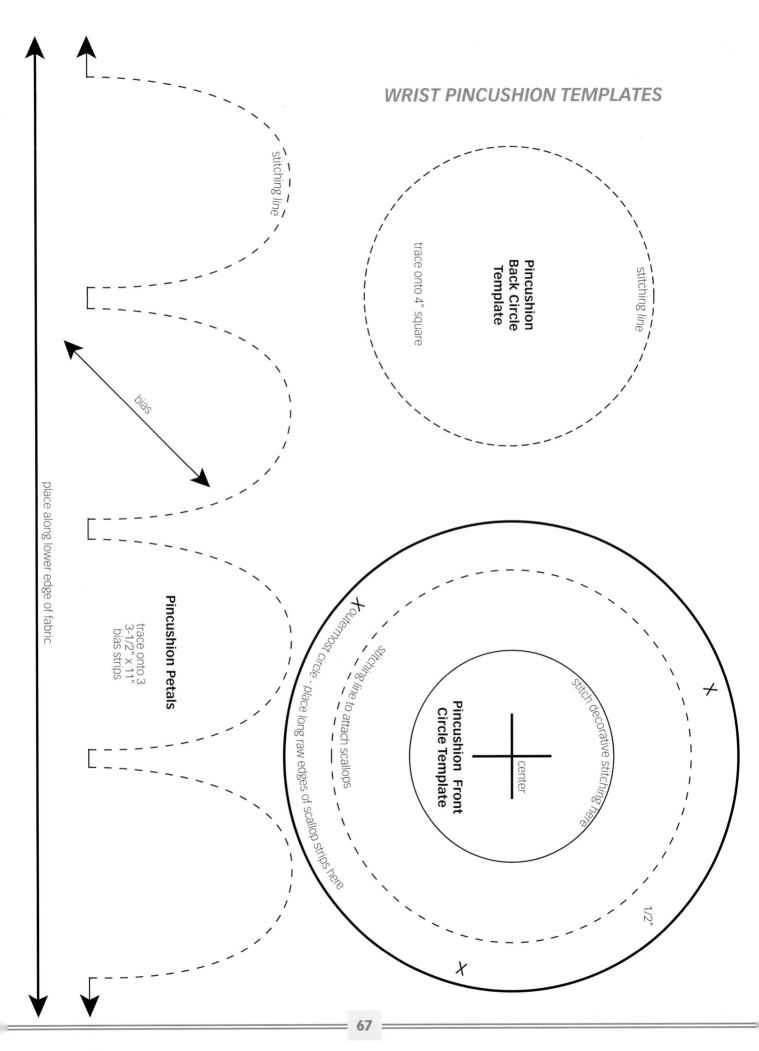

stitching line

Pincushion
Back Circle
Template

trace onto 4" square

stitching line

bias

place along lower edge of fabric

Pincushion Petals
trace onto 3
3-1/2" x 11"
bias strips

X outermost circle - place long raw edges of scallop strips here

stitching line to attach scallops

Pincushion Front
Circle Template

center

stitch decorative stitching here

1/2"

X

X

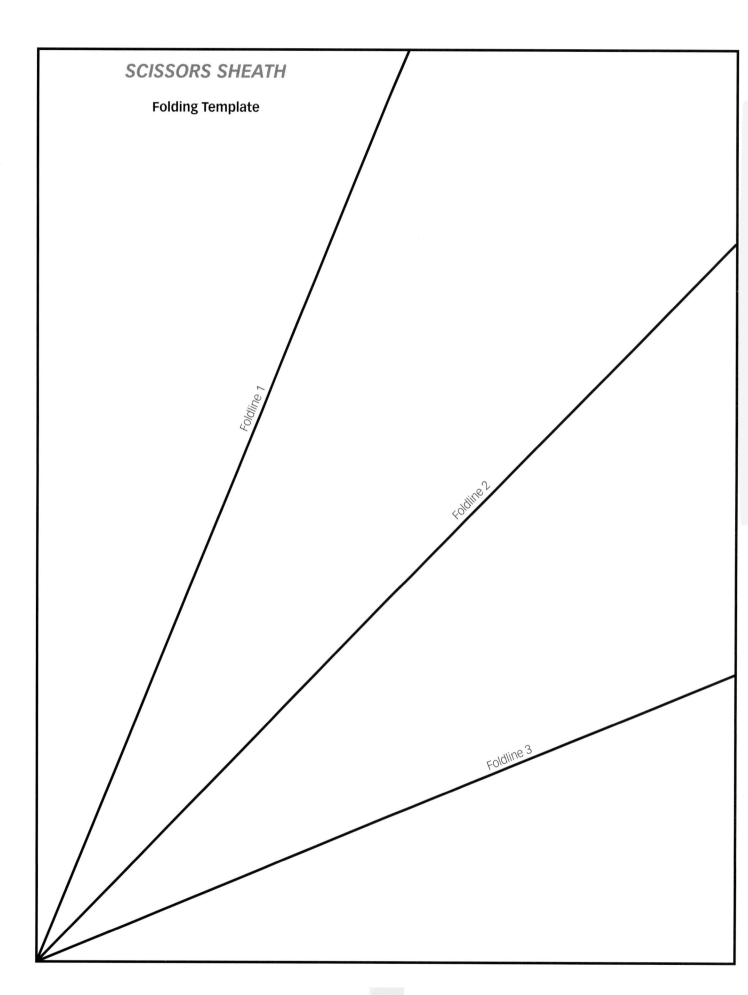

SCISSORS SHEATH

Folding Template

Foldline 1

Foldline 2

Foldline 3

White Linen Blend (43/44" wide) **2/3 yard**

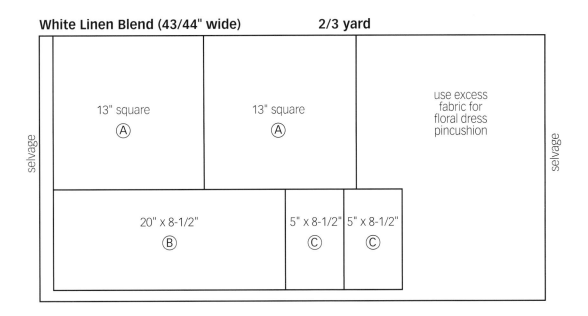

selvage

13" square
Ⓐ

13" square
Ⓐ

use excess
fabric for
floral dress
pincushion

20" x 8-1/2"
Ⓑ

5" x 8-1/2"
Ⓒ

5" x 8-1/2"
Ⓒ

selvage

Lavender Linen Blend (43/44" wide) **One yard**

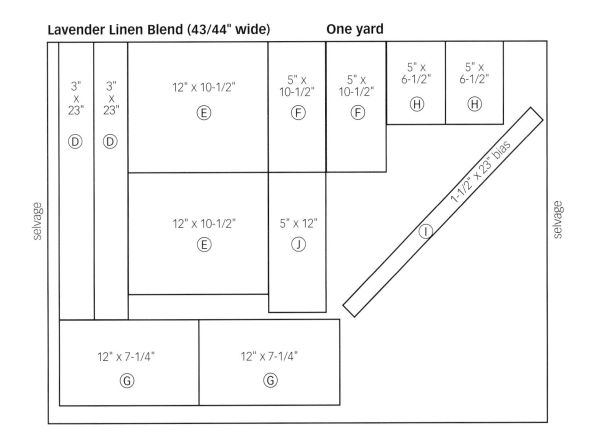

selvage

3"
x
23"
Ⓓ

3"
x
23"
Ⓓ

12" x 10-1/2"
Ⓔ

5" x
10-1/2"
Ⓕ

5" x
10-1/2"
Ⓕ

5" x
6-1/2"
Ⓗ

5" x
6-1/2"
Ⓗ

12" x 10-1/2"
Ⓔ

5" x 12"
Ⓙ

1-1/2" x 23" bias
Ⓘ

12" x 7-1/4"
Ⓖ

12" x 7-1/4"
Ⓖ

selvage

CUTTING GUIDE
SEWING PURSE

Green Linen Blend (43/44" wide)   **3/4 yard**

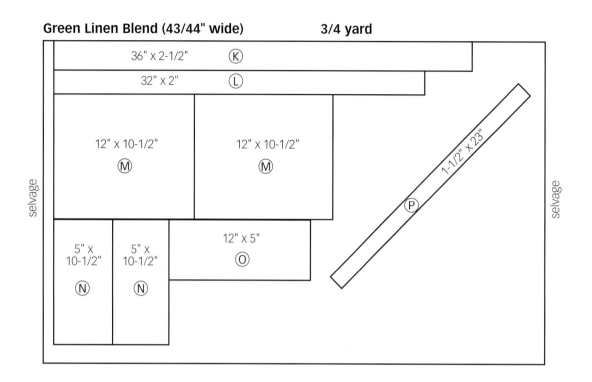

CUTTING GUIDE
ELEGANT ORGANIZER

Candy Pink Silk Dupioni (45" wide)   **7/8 yard**

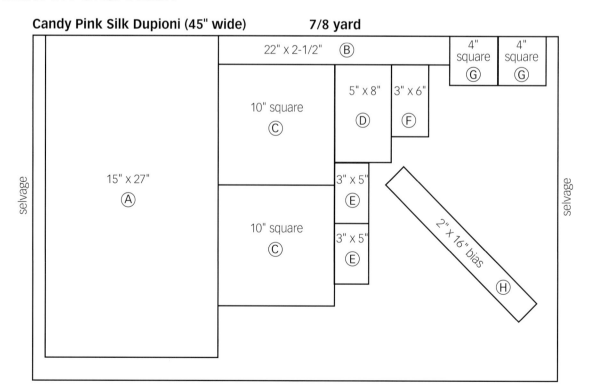

Natural Linen Blend (43/44" wide)   **3/4 yard**

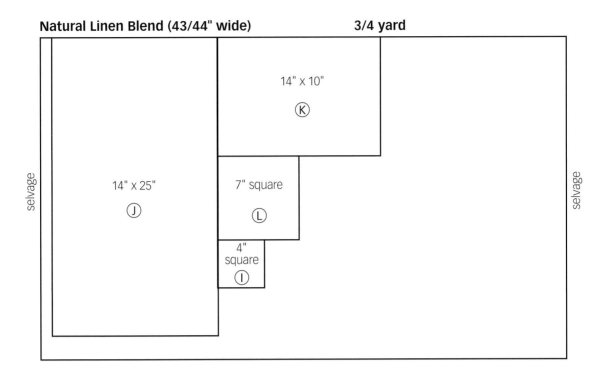

Candy Pink/Brown Silk Dupioni Check (45" wide)   **7/8 yard**

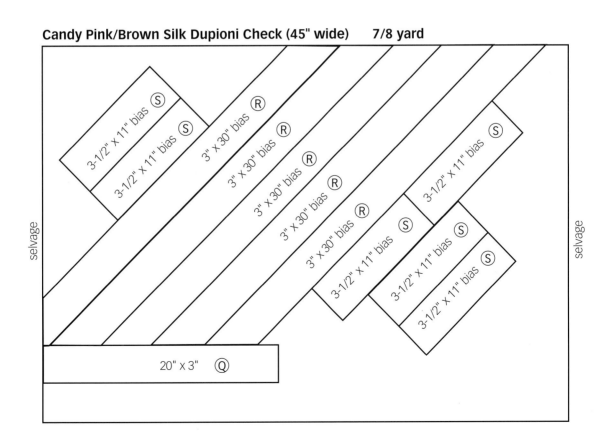

Sources

Fabrics, laces, trims, buttons, thread, as well as an extensive list of sewing supplies and embroidery CD collections can be purchased from the following:

Martha Pullen Company, Inc.
149 Old Big Cove Road
Brownsboro, AL 35761

256.533.9586 / 800.547.4176

www.marthapullen.com
www.sewbeautifulmag.com

Supplies not available from Martha Pullen Company may be purchased from your local fabric store or machine dealership.

Contact your local machine dealership for feet and specialty machine accessories.